Frank Damazio

The Power of Spiritual Alignment

Living According to the Seven Firsts of Jesus

CITY BIBLE
PUBLISHING

Portland, Oregon, U.S.A.

The
POWER of
Spiritual
Alignment

Almost daily someone asks me, "What is the key to finding fruitfulness in ministry?" My starting place and reply always centers around the concept of "submission," in one regard or another. *To Align* is the essence of that biblical fundamental, and Frank Damazio identifies these priorities and how they may be understood and applied.

— *JACK W. HAYFORD, Litt.D., Pastor/Chancellor,*
  The Church On the Way, The King' s Seminary

◆

The great struggle of the Christian life will inevitably begin and end when one recognizes and wholly embraces the absolute authority of the King-dom of God and its values. In the post Post-Modern world, we are virtually inundated by a tsunami of demands upon our time. Dr. Frank Damazio's extensive experiences in pastoral, educational and leadership-mentoring ministries have placed him at the forefront of a few who articulate biblically sound and refreshingly practical insights essential for Christian growth and maturity. You will cherish the message in this book, because no Christian will ever outgrow the need for its central theme.

— *BISHOP JOSEPH L. GARLINGTON, Sr., PhD.*
  Covenant Church of Pittsburgh

THE POWER OF SPIRITUAL ALIGNMENT

Just when you thought you knew all that Jesus meant with His significant teachings, a book like "*The Power of Spiritual Alignment*" comes along to put it in an all new, powerfully practical perspective. To me, Frank Damazio is one of the most practical Christian authors of our day and it shows in this timely challenge.

— *DR. DICK EASTMAN, International President, Every Home for Christ*

You'll want to read Pastor Frank Damazio's new book twice—the second time with a Bible and pen in hand. Then get ready to enter into God's best for every area of your life. Highly recommended!

— *LUIS PALAU, world-renowned evangelist, broadcaster, and author*

Frank invites us to consider seven core values which enable us to live with purpose and satisfaction. I heartily recommend *The Power of Spiritual Alignment* for your edification.

— *JOE ALDRICH*

Thank you, Frank for encouraging us and helping us to (re)align our lives according to the "firsts" of Scripture. There really is power in spiritual alignment! I feel that chapter five is worth the price of the book! Passion for God seems to be both a better motivator and a more consistent possibility than desperation. I found myself drawn to a fresh passion for God as I read that chapter. May it be widely read and applied!

— *DENNIS FUQUA, Executive Director, International Renewal Ministries*

Here is another good book by Frank Damazio. It is different from any of his other books which are really textbooks and resource manuals. This one is different. It is very practical and not so much theological or parabolic. There is plenty of material for sermons for any in pastoral or teaching ministry. Again, it is worth a place in any minister's library.

— *KEVIN J. CONNER, Waverley Christian Fellowship*

◆

This book is a strategic resource to assist us in aligning our lives with the values of the kingdom while living in the midst of a secular society. Frank's teaching has the potential to be a catalyst to ensure that you place "first things first" in your life and ministry.

— *MARK CONNER, Senior Minister, Waverley Christian Fellowship, Melbourne, Australia*

◆

What we put first determines what is added to our lives. This book will challenge every believer to examine their priorities and align their lives with God's purposes.

— *BRIAN HOUSTON, Senior Pastor, Hillsong Church*

◆

First things first! Frank Damazio's *The Power of Spiritual Alignment* equips the reader to do just that. From the perspective of the seven "firsts" of Jesus, the author invites us to discover the power that lies with aligning our lives with the Word. A properly serviced and aligned vehicle maintains its highest level of performance. The abundant life promised by Jesus will be lived by those who have discovered *The Power of Spiritual Alignment*!

— *TOMMY TENNEY, Author of "The God Chasers"*

WORDS OF PRAISE FOR
THE POWER OF SPIRITUAL ALIGNMENT

The Power of Spiritual Alignment is one of the most powerful and timely books I have read in a long time. It is impacting and life-changing! Every believer needs to read this book to help get their Christian walk properly aligned.

— *CINDY JACOBS, Generals of Intercession*

◆

Frank Damazio offers sharp and fresh insight on the value of an ordered life. The master of keeping the main things the main things effectively communicates important ideas that will help shape a new generation of leaders. When Frank Damazio speaks, I listen closely.

— *TED HAGGARD, Senior Pastor, New Life Church,*
Colorado Springs, Colorado

◆

PUBLISHED BY CITY BIBLE PUBLISHING
9200 NE FREMONT, PORTLAND, OREGON 97220

PRINTED IN U.S.A.

City Bible Publishing is a ministry of City Bible Church and is dedicated to serving the local church and its leaders through the production and distribution of quality restoration materials.

It is our prayer that these materials, proven in the context of the local church, will equip leaders in exalting the Lord and extending His kingdom.

For a free catalog of additional resources from City Bible Publishing please call 1-800-777-6057 or visit our web site at www.citybiblepublishing.com.

The Power of Spiritual Alignment

ISBN: 1-886849-87-0

◆

This book is dedicated to...

Albie Pearson, the one man who brought spiritual alignment to my life. Thank you, Albie, for your deep love and enduring faith in me and in so many other young leaders. May great blessings and abundant grace rest upon every area of your life.

Table of Contents

The outer appearance of the Tabernacle of Moses was not eye-appealing; it was made of badger skin. In stark contrast, the inside of the Tabernacle was decorated with intricately woven veils and lovely tapestries. The Tabernacle is symbolic of the Holy Spirit's continuous weaving together of beautiful qualities in our character as He brings our lives into Kingdom alignment.

Giving Him the first day is symbolic of allowing Him to take first place in the other six days. It is a way of tithing out lives and our time so that every other area of our lives can be fully blessed.

◆

A special thanks to those who made this book possible...

Karen Kaufman for your gifted editing, your hard work and your patience. Thank you for making me look so good!

Cheryl Bolton for your work on all the details of getting this book published, and Alida Little for keeping the rest of my life administrated so that I have time to write. You both go above and beyond the call of duty. Thank you.

◆

Introduction

Laws for Living

In a Peanuts cartoon, Lucy philosophizes to Charlie Brown: "Charlie Brown, life is a lot like a deck chair. Some place it to see where they've been and some so they can see where they are at the present." Charlie Brown sighs, "I can't even get mine unfolded."

Perhaps you feel like Charlie Brown, wondering how to unfold your deck chair in order to get a right perspective on your past, present and future. If so, keep reading. In this book we will delve into the Gospel of Matthew to discover the seven "first things" that Jesus said we must do if we want to align our lives with His priorities. These "first things," or core values, are a guiding rule for living successfully with others; they are the bottom line for a victorious spiritual life.

In a time when many people are aimlessly meandering about the earth as wandering generalities, those who have implemented these "first things" have become purposeful possibilities. By obeying Jesus with the "first things," they are able to push all non-essentials out of the way.

Stephen Covey, author of *First Things First Everyday*, says, "The main thing is to keep the main thing the main thing." But many people do not know the main thing of life. Do you? What is the main thing in your life? What is the "first thing" that pushes all non-essentials out of your way? I believe that until your life has been aligned with God's Law of First Things, it will be almost impossible to fulfill your main purpose, which is to be the focus of your life.

An ancient adage says, "If you want to defeat them, distract them." The world, the flesh and the devil are all masterfully crafty at distracting us and causing us to lose our grasp on the first things we should live by. And if we allow *second* things to become first, we will lose both the second and the first things. Our challenge then is to be like Jesus who knew His "law of firsts"—and did not deviate from it.

THE LAW OF FIRST THINGS,
THE SEVEN FIRSTS OF JESUS

The word "first" in the Greek means first in time and number, first in rank and value—in other words, the most important. The dictionary defines first as "foremost in place, preceding all others in number, the first thing; that which is before anything else; the beginning, the first move, fresh start; the starting point the place of new departure, a new day."

As we observe the Law of First Things as taught by the Lord, we will be using the following seven key "first" Scriptures from the words of Jesus:

1. Matthew 6:33: "But seek *first* the kingdom of God and His righteousness, and all these things shall be added to you."

2. Matthew 7:4,5: "Or how can you say to your brother, 'Let me remove the speck from your eye'; and look, a plank is in your own eye? Hypocrite! *First* remove the plank from your own eye, and then you will see clearly to remove the speck out of your brother's eye."

3. Matthew 5:24,25: "Leave your gift there before the altar, and go your way. *First* be reconciled to your brother, and then come and offer your gift. Agree with your adversary quickly, while you are on the way with him, lest your adversary deliver you to the judge, the judge hand you over to the officer, and you are thrown into prison."

4. Matthew 12:29: "Or how can one enter a strong man's house and plunder his goods, unless he *first* binds the strong man? And then he will plunder his house.

5. Matthew 22:36-38: "'Teacher, which is the great commandment in the law?' Jesus said to him, 'You shall love the Lord your God with all your heart, with all your soul, and with all your mind. This is the *first* and great commandment.'"

6. Matthew 23:26: "Blind Pharisee, *first* cleanse the inside of the cup and dish, that the outside of them may be clean also."

7. Matthew 28:1: "Now after the Sabbath, as the *first* day of the week began to dawn, Mary Magdalene and the other Mary came to see the tomb."

The Lord Jesus establishes the Law of First Things in at least these seven Scriptures. And even though other first Scriptures could be referenced here, I consider these to be Christ's seven foundational first things.

EVERY MINISTRY MUST HAVE A LAW OF FIRST THINGS

Although this book will primarily look at the first things of Jesus, every successful ministry must have a set of core values to build upon. These first things are essential to the ministry's foundation and lasting integrity.

For example, early in his ministry, Billy Graham conferred with Cliff Barrows and Grady Wilson, close friends and partners in the work of the Lord, to write what they later called the *Modesto Manifesto* (because they wrote it in Modesto, California). This manifesto was to represent their laws for living, the first things they would adhere to in their personal lives and ministry. They decided:

1. Money would be handled wisely and with accountability. Graham would draw a salary and not live by the offerings.

2. Billy Graham would never travel by himself. From that day forward he never met with, ate with or spoke alone with a woman other than his own wife while traveling.

3. They would work with the local churches and never criticize pastors or churches, but would instead cooperate with all of them.

4. They would never exaggerate their successes or claim higher attendance numbers than they had actually experienced.

These four decisions became their laws for living, the Kingdom priorities they would commit to throughout all their years in the ministry. During discussions, debates or disagreements, the four laws of the *Modesto Manifesto*—which they had established as young men—were used to solve their problems.

And then there was Hudson Taylor, the famed missionary to China, who cultivated his first laws for living during what he termed his "hidden years." After six years of dedicated service in China, Taylor's failing health forced his return to England. He was merely 29 years old and his wife was only 24. At home in England, Hudson and his wife resided on a very dreary street in a poor part of London, cut off from the work they loved. Yet without those hidden years, how could the vision and enthusiasm of youth have matured for the leadership that would earmark Hudson Taylor's life?

It was during that hidden time that Hudson would hone out his laws for living, his first things which would later provide the foundation for many years of ministry. He learned to live by faith, making a commitment to deepen his devotions to daily prayer and dependence upon God only. He became faithful to the smallest detail—committed to what he could not see but could only believe. He formed the conviction of first praying for more laborers before seeking out more missionaries. He learned a law: prayer first and always first—for money, for workers, for facilities, for decisions. For the rest of his life, Hudson Taylor would spend a major portion of each day first in prayer. He would never ask for offerings; he would only pray and believe God for the financial needs to be met. He made a commitment to the first thing—that God would be first and everything else would fall into second place. Hudson Taylor became the father of faith missions, which was unheard of in his day. He taught his team how to use the principles of first things: first prayer, first God, first your own heart and soul. First obey principle and never fear man.

Another man who understood the Law of First Things was Winston Churchill. When he became the Prime Minister of England, Churchill delivered a very short speech to the House of Commons, a speech that reflected his ability to have a single focus, a clear aim—laws for first things that were non-negotiable. In very few words, Churchill set the tone and spirit that England would need in order to win the victory over Germany:

> I would say to the House as I have said to those who have joined this government. I have nothing to offer but blood, toil, tears and sweat. You asked, 'What is your policy?' I will say it is to wage war by sea, land and air with all our might and with all the strength God can give us. This is our policy. You ask, 'What is our aim?' I can answer in one word. It is victory. Victory at all costs. Victory in spite of all terror. Victory however long and hard the road may be. For without victory there is no survival.

Winston Churchill, Hudson Taylor and Billy Graham are three examples of people who learned the Law of First Things—and they never deviated from it. Rather than allowing their lives to be driven by circumstances or moods, they kept the main thing the main thing and became purposeful, passionate people with enormous impact.

What about you? Do you want to make a difference in this world? Do you want to live a life filled with meaning and purpose? If you are committed to changing your life and filling it with the glory of God and the purposes of Christ, then the pages of this book will have life-changing influence upon you. Every one of the first things of Jesus will lead you to keeping the main thing the main thing. Like those who have traveled God's path before us, you and I must first find that main thing before we can maintain it, but we must start with the Law of First Things first. I look forward to discovering your main thing with you as you journey through the pages that follow.

PASTOR FRANK DAMAZIO
City Bible Church
Portland, Oregon

First Seek the Kingdom
Aligning Your Priorities

*"But seek first the kingdom of God and His righteousness,
and all these things shall be added to you."*
—Matthew 6:33

On Tuesday, September 17th, 1998, a power shortage at an AT&T switching center crashed the computer system, leaving more than one million New Yorkers without phones. The power failure forced all New York airports to shut down for seven hours, which caused delays throughout the country. Several hundred thousand people were affected. How did this happen? A broken part? No. Negligence! Two men who ran the switching station ignored both audio and visual warning alarms signaling that the computer was losing power and was about to crash.

Likewise, we can begin to lose power by neglecting the Holy Spirit's warning signals concerning our core values. Consider King Saul in 1 Samuel 28. He maintained his position of anointing but lost the power of his anointing when he became more concerned about his own kingdom than God's. None of us are exempt from power shortages. Our anointings can leak right out of our spiritual spinal cords and cause the power we supply to the rest of the Body to shut down if we neglect the first thing of seeking God first. As a matter fact, like King Saul, we may be the last ones to recognize our loss of power while the hundreds or thousands we were born to influence stand by watching and waiting.

SEEK FIRST THE KINGDOM OF GOD

In Matthew 6:33 the Lord Jesus gives us one of the "first things" that we will be delving into in this chapter. "Set your heart *first* on His Kingdom and His goodness and all these things will come to you as a matter of course" (*J.B. Phillips,* emphasis added). Another translation says, "But you must make His Kingdom and uprightness before Him your greatest care and all will be yours over and above" (*Godspeed*). The Damazio translation might read, "If you put God *first* in all your decisions and choices, you will have all the power you need to do what you could never have the power to do in your own strength."

Putting God first means dethroning anything that stands between you and the Lord. Jesus explained, "No one can serve two masters; for either he will hate the one and love the other, or else he will be loyal to the one and desire the other or despise the other. You cannot serve God and mammon" (Matt. 6:24). A woman once said to the famed missionary E. Stanley Jones, "Dr. Jones, you are obsessed with the kingdom of God." His reply, "I wish that were true, because that would be a magnificent obsession."

But becoming obsessed with the kingdom of God, means staying on guard for warning signs of trouble—it means routinely and painstakingly inventorying our lives. Socrates said of life appraisal, "An unexamined life is not worth living." We are seeking to appraise our lives by studying the words of Jesus. The seven first things stated by Jesus are a measuring rod for us to evaluate our quality of life as well as our fulfillment in life.

My intention is to ignite your passion for God and to encourage you to return to your first love, which is the Lord Jesus Himself. If you serve the Lord according to His Law of First Things, you will live a profitable and fulfilling life. Let's begin by looking at what we mean by first.

FIRST

To place something first means it must be the first in time and number, first in rank and value, the most important. To place something first means that it becomes foremost in any place of your life, preceding all others in number. The first thing is the most important thing. Keep first the kingdom of God.

The following are some different Bible translations so that you can begin to meditate with me concerning Matthew 6:33:

Amplified Bible: "But seek (aim at and strive after) first of all His kingdom and His righteousness (His way of doing and being right), and then all these things taken together will be given you besides."

J.B. Phillips: "Set your heart first on His kingdom and His goodness and all these things will come to you as a matter of course."

Wuest: "But be seeking first the kingdom and His goodness and all these things, all of them, shall be added to you."

Weymouth: "But make His kingdom and righteousness your chief aim and then these things shall all be given you in addition."

Young's Literal: "But seek ye first the reign of God and His righteousness and all these shall be added to you."

Godspeed: "But you must make His kingdom and uprightness before Him, your greatest care and all will be yours over and above."

Barclay: "Make the Kingdom of God and life in loyalty to Him, the object of all your endeavor, and you will get all these other things as well."

THE IMPORTANCE OF RENEWING A KINGDOM LIFESTYLE

George Barna, while doing research on American values, made the following comment:

> When individuals are single-minded in their devotion to God, then commitment to His ways and His principles becomes much deeper, much more intense. Once they have made an enduring and serious commitment, then the peripherals don't matter as much.

When we renew our commitment to the Kingdom lifestyle and Kingdom values, those things about our lives that have formerly been outside the lordship of Christ should start to align with His Word, with biblical priorities. Seeking first the kingdom of God begins to shape our moral, ethical and philosophical convictions and directly affects our responses to pain and hardship. It fosters strength in times of temptation and spawns courage and faith when we face impossible odds. A Kingdom commitment dictates our lifestyles and gives meaning and significance to all of our relationships. It even affects the kinds of relationships we seek.

The word "seek" that Jesus uses in Matthew 6:33 implies being absorbed in the search for, a persevering and strenuous effort to obtain, to be constantly seeking after that which is important. To seek means that we earnestly pursue that which God has promised us in order to fulfill our destinies and enjoy our lives. Psalm 16: 11 says, "You will show me the path of life; in Your presence is fullness of joy; at Your right hand are pleasures forevermore." Think of that: God wants you to enjoy the journey! And enjoyment suggests worry-free living. Matthew 6:25 explains:

> "Therefore I say to you, do not worry about your life, what you will eat or what you will drink; nor about your body, what you will put on. Is not life more than food and the body more than clothing?"

WRONG SEEKING MEANS WORRY-LADEN LIVING

Seeking the wrong things results in worry. The word "worry" comes from an old German word meaning to strangle or choke. In other words, worry is a mental and emotional strangulation. It is a thin stream of fear that trickles through the mind which, if encouraged, will cut a channel so wide that all other positive thoughts are drained out. Worry and faith cannot coexist; one will drive the other out of our lives.

God does not worry. Therefore, the Lord Jesus instructs us to seek first the kingdom of God because it is a worry-free kingdom. Worry is sin; it distrusts the promises and providence of God. Worry is irreverent;

it fails to recognize God as the Master Controller of all things. Worry is also irrelevant; it doesn't change anything. Worry is irresponsible; it burns up our spiritual energy and lures us into a realm of unbelief that will drain us of spiritual vision. Worry is unreasonable because as people of faith, we do not live in the realm of unbelief. Worry is the opposite of contentment, and we are ordered by Scripture to live contented lives (see Phil. 4:11,12; 1 Tim. 6: 6-8).

Contentment isn't getting what you want—it's being satisfied with what you have. Usually worry comes because we have set our hearts on things that can be seen, on material things. Our real problems are concealed from us by seeking after new

> "Contentment isn't getting what you want— it's being satisfied with what you have."

ways of getting what we desire rather than what God wants us to have. We buy things from one another that we do not want at prices we cannot pay on terms we cannot meet because of advertising we do not believe. Therefore, the first step toward letting go and letting God provide what He wants us to have is realizing that most of the problems we fret about are bound to us by the hold we have upon them.

A story is told of an expedition of scientists who were on a mission to capture a particular species of monkeys in the jungles of Africa. It was important that the monkeys be brought back alive and unharmed. Using their knowledge of monkey ways, the scientists devised a trap consisting of a small jar with a long, narrow neck. Into the jar was placed a handful of nuts. Several of these jars were staked out, while the scientists returned to their camp, confident of catching the monkeys.

Scenting the nuts in the bottle, a monkey would thrust its paw into the long neck and take a fistful of nuts. But when the monkey tried to withdraw the prize, it discovered that its clenched fist would not pass through the narrow neck of the bottle. So, the monkey was trapped in the anchored bottle, unable to escape with its booty, and yet unwilling to let it go. When the scientists returned, they easily took the monkeys captive. We may smile at the monkeys, thinking how foolish they were, but in some respects we are just like them. We cling to the very things that hold us back, remaining captive through sheer unwillingness to let go.[1]

Right Seeking Results in Peaceful Living

As believers, we must make right choices, because choosing to seek the right things results in the peace of God. When we seek the Kingdom first, our seeking of other things from the Father will come through humble and submissive prayer—without worry and without a false estimate of what is necessary for living a properly aligned life. Because we have prayerfully sought the Father, we have the peaceful assurance that whether or not we obtain what we have asked, we are being protected and provided for in what we receive.

Philippians 4:6,7 says that we are to "be anxious for nothing, but in everything by prayer and supplication, with thanksgiving, let your requests be made known to God; and the peace of God, which surpasses all understanding, will guard your hearts and minds through Christ Jesus."

The more we seek after God through His Word and through prayer, the more we will be able to trust Him and believe that He loves us. First Peter 5:7 says that you and I are to be "casting all your care upon Him, for He cares for you."

But trust is a choice, and until we make the choice to trust in God's faithfulness, we cannot walk in dependence upon His character or be in alignment with His Kingdom will for our lives. Lamentations 3:22,23 says, "Through the Lord's mercies we are not consumed, because His compassions fail not. They are new every morning. Great is Your faithfulness." True believers seek first God's kingdom—not simply to refrain from the pursuit of temporal things, but to replace such pursuits with goals of greater significance, such as reliance upon God.

Seeking First the Kingdom Is Seeing Life God's Way

Believers should renew the focus of their lives to seek first the kingdom of God. "Seeking first the Kingdom" is not just a good Christian phrase. It is a principle and truth that each one of us can apply in very specific ways. Watchman Nee said, "A spiritual man is not a man born again, but a man born again and walking in alignment." We need to learn how to walk in alignment with the kingdom of God, with a single eye and a single focus:

> The lamp of the body is the eye. If therefore your eye be in single focus, pure and sound, your whole body will be well lighted. But if your eye be diseased, your whole body will be full of darkness" (Matt. 6:22,23, Wuest).

The Lord is not speaking here of the physical eye but of the inner spiritual eye, or value focus. To have a single eye is to have an eye without ulterior motives, one that is free from inner discord, upright and pure. In Scripture, the eye refers to a particular way of seeing things and actually speaks of your focus on life. You may have an out-of-focus look on life and need to have an eye adjustment in order to develop a single eye. If so, run to Doctor Jesus and He will help you to see things from God's point of view, not from a self-centered or a worldly point of view.

Do you want to have a joyful heart and healthy bones? Do you want to know what your calling is? Listen to the words of the Great Physician:

> Proverbs 15:30: The light of the eyes rejoices the heart, and a good report makes the bones healthy.

> Ephesians 1:18: The eyes of your understanding being enlightened; that you may know what is the hope of His calling, what are the riches of the glory of His inheritance in the saints.

SEEKING FIRST THE KINGDOM IS GIVING GOD THE HIGHEST PLACE

When our focus is on seeking the Kingdom first, God will control the highest place in our lives. Our love for Him will be the motivation for all that we say, think and do.

For example, in Ephesians 3:17, the apostle Paul prays, "That Christ might dwell in your hearts through faith; that you, being rooted and grounded in love [might grow in Him]." The word "dwell" comes from two words in the Greek. One means "to live in a home"; the other means "down." Paul is praying that our Lord might live in our hearts as His home, that He might feel at home in our hearts. In other words, Paul is praying, "That Christ may finally settle down and feel comfortably at home in your hearts."

Hudson Taylor, the English missionary doctor to China, knew how to give God the highest place in his heart. In 1854 he recorded the following statement in his journal:

> Well do I remember how in the gladness of my heart I poured out my soul before God. Again and again confessing my grateful love to Him who had done everything for me, who had saved me when I had given up all hope and even desire for salvation. I besought Him to give me some work to do for Him as an outlet for love and gratitude....Well do I remember as I put myself, my life, my friends, my all upon the altar, the deep solemnity that came over my soul with the assurance that my offering was accepted. The presence of God became unutterably real and blessed, and I remember...stretching myself on the ground and lying there before Him with unspeakable awe and unspeakable joy. For what service I was accepted I knew not, but a deep consciousness that I was not my own took possession of me which has never since been effaced. [2]

To place God on the highest place means to cleanse our lives. For each one of us the high places that need cleansing are different, but in any area where we have found our worth and reliance outside of God, that high place must be cleansed. To give God the highest place is to align your goals and ambitions with the Kingdom so that in all of your success, God is glorified.

In the Old Testament, the high places were occupied by many different gods that had to be removed by the righteous kings who would come in and cleanse the high places (see Deut. 33:29; Judges 5:18; 2 Sam. 22:34; 1 Kings 11:7; 12:31; 14:23,24; 15:14; 22:43). And even though Israel struggled with maintaining obedience to God, when He was restored to the high place a new government was instituted over the land and a new blessing came upon the people.

So it is in our lives. As we restore the Lord to the high places, the blessing of God will rule and reign over every aspect of our lives—our marriages, jobs, children, finances, health, friendships and other relationships. To seek first the kingdom of God is to restore God to the high place (see 1 Kings 3:2-4; Ps. 7:7; 7:17; 9:2; 57:2; Mark 5:7; 2 Cor. 10:5; Phil. 3:14).

SEEKING FIRST THE KINGDOM IS HUNGERING AFTER GOD

To seek first the Kingdom is to have an appetite for spiritual things. The apostle Paul tells us that, "the natural man does not receive the things of the Spirit of God, for they are foolishness to him; nor can he know them, because they are spiritually discerned. But he who is spiritual judges all things, yet he himself is rightly judged by no one. For 'who has known the mind of the Lord that he may instruct Him?' But we have the mind of Christ" (1 Cor. 2:14-16).

When we are walking in alignment with God, our appetite for spiritual things is constantly growing. Rightly aligned believers have a hunger, a thirst, a desire, a passion, an appetite for the things of the Holy Spirit—things such as prayer, worship, reading the Word, sharing the gospel, fellowshipping with believers and interceding for others.

In Psalm 73:25 King David asks, "Whom have I in heaven but You? And there is none upon earth that I desire besides You." Let me ask you, dear reader, who and what has captivated your heart? Whatever you set your affections and desires upon will become reality in your life. We all have time to do the things we really want to do. Likewise, most of us can manage to find a way to acquire the things we really want to have. Our calendars and checkbooks tell a lot more about us than our words do. They tell who, what and where we have invested our lives.

SEEKING FIRST THE KINGDOM IS WHOLLY FOLLOWING GOD

The words "wholly followed" are often used to describe someone who has put God first in his or her life. Caleb was one who wholly followed. At the age of 85 he was still spiritually alert, committed and ready for the challenge. He lived for God wholeheartedly, with nothing held back.

Some people say that the best way to live your life is to write your epitaph and live your life according to what you want written about you. What greater compliment than to read, "This person wholly followed the Lord. Everything about him or her spoke of Kingdom passion and Kingdom values." (See 2 Tim. 4:6-7.)

I once knew a woman who lived to the ripe old age of 103. At 101 years young, this beloved lady's mind was overtaken with dementia. She didn't know where she was, but she still knew whose she was. Her heart was so full of the Word of God that Scripture dripped continuously from her lips, even in her sleep. When she could no longer recognize her family members, she could still speak of the One whom she had wholly followed for more than a century.

SEEKING FIRST THE KINGDOM IS COMMUNING WITH GOD FIRST

"Good morning, Lord," will be our waking words—whether spoken out loud or in our hearts—when our lives are rightly aligned with the Kingdom. These words imply a wholehearted devotion to Him. Devotion belongs to the inner life and lives in the closet. It belongs to the person whose thoughts and feelings are lovingly loyal to God, no matter what the cost. Devotion is the genesis of the whole matter of activity and strength of the most energetic, exhaustless and untiring nature; it is the result of waiting upon God. There is no greater way to increase your love for the Lord than to converse with Him at the beginning and end of every day. God loves the sound of your voice. He longs to make Himself known to you and to empower your life. Can you hear Him beckoning you now:

1 Chronicles 28:9: As for you, [insert your name here], know the God of your father, and serve Him with a loyal heart and with a willing mind; for the Lord searches all hearts and understands all the intent of the thoughts. If **YOU** seek Him, He will be found by you; but if you forsake Him, He will cast you off forever" (emphasis added).

Isaiah 40:31: But those who wait on the Lord shall renew their strength; they shall mount up with wings like eagles, they shall run and not be weary, they shall walk and not faint.

Our ability and discipline with God may begin first with minutes and then increase to the point were we might give as much as an hour each morning and even more throughout the day. Eventually everything we do should be in obedience to our communication with God so that we are praying "without ceasing" (1 Thess. 5:17). Have you yet made your prayerful first thing a reality and the first part of your day? Communion with God will be stolen from you if you do not hide yourself in your prayer closet prior to all other daily activity. A heart that daily seeks first the kingdom of God is a heart that is ready for every challenge and will respond properly to any kind of abuse, temptation or trial.

> "A heart that daily seeks first the kingdom of God is a heart that is ready for every challenge and will respond properly to any kind of abuse, temptation or trial."

SEEKING FIRST THE KINGDOM IS FOLLOWING AND HONORING JESUS IN ALL THINGS

We've all seen the "What Would Jesus Do?" bracelets and possibly even read the book *In His Steps*, from which this phrase is taken. It speaks of a life that totally follows the Lord Jesus' example in every situation. But surrendering to His will in everything means being completely aligned with the Word of God. Thomas A. Kempis, the German mystic said, "But whoever would fully and feelingly understand the words of Christ must endeavor to conform his life wholly to the life of Christ."

Conforming our lives wholly to the life of Christ means putting Christ in the center of our values, choices, gifts, capacities and personal performance. It means becoming persons of flawless character and integrity and inviting the Spirit of God to empower us to honor Jesus. "In everything we do"—in every act, every decision, every move and every motion—is a great challenge for each one of us as believers, but nonetheless that is our challenge.

Matthew 11:29,30 assures us that when we chose to yoke ourselves with Jesus, the burden that we take on to become more like Him is a light burden, not a heavy one. He promises that God's hand will be upon us for good and not evil. God's Holy Spirit will continually be working with us to increase our character and integrity, to forgive us of our sins and to help us in our weaknesses. The Holy Spirit knows when we grieve Jesus, when we disobey the Scriptures and do not honor the Lord. Nevertheless, He is quick to forgive us and quick to pick us up, reminding us that we are His anointed children and that He will pour out His grace upon us so that we will have the strength to honor Him in everything we do (see Phil. 1:20,21).

SEEKING FIRST THE KINGDOM IS REMOVING ALL CLUTTER

To seek first the Kingdom is to remove all the clutter that gets between me and God (see Rom. 12:1,2). Aiden Wilson Tozer, who lived from 1897–1963, understood well the principle of "cleaning out the clutter." This country boy, without formal education, became one of the greatest American pastors, writers and leaders of Southside Alliance Church in Chicago from 1928–1959. As a pastor, Tozer did virtually no administrative work or pastoral counseling. He invested all of his time in prayer, meditation and the Word of God. The list of books he wrote is lengthy, but his classic is entitled *The Pursuit of God*. One of A. W. Tozer's prayers reads:

Father, I want to know thee, but my coward heart fears to give up its toys. I cannot part with them without inward bleeding, and I do not try to hide from Thee the terror of the parting. I come trembling, but I do come. Please root from my heart all those things which I have cherished so long and which have become a very part of my living self, so that Thou mayest enter and dwell there without a rival. Then shalt Thou make the place of Thy feet glorious. Then shall my heart have no need of the sun to shine in it, for Thyself wilt be the light of it, and there shall be no night there. In Jesus' name. Amen.[3]

Clutter can be anything that crowds out Jesus in your life. It can refer to thoughts, activities, relationships, work, television and things that gorge you to the point that Jesus is not first. Clutter is not in and of itself inherently sinful. For instance, I've noticed with raising four children that even our children's activities, which are good, can become clutter. My lovely wife and I have to discipline ourselves as to how many sports the kids will play, how many instruments they will learn, how many activities they will participate in, how many friends they are allowed to invite to our home on week nights, how many church and youth outings they will attend. If we are not watchful, even these things can threaten to clutter our spiritual worlds.

All of us should be careful about how much we work, how much we play, how many friendships we have and what we do with every minute of the day. Clutter of unnecessary activity, things, habits and attitudes needs to be removed by the wisdom of the Holy Spirit. I don't know about you, but I'm thinking about having a spiritual garage sale to clean out the clutter that I've collected.

Now what about you? Would you be willing right this minute to just stop and allow the Holy Spirit to show you some of the clutter that needs to be removed in your life? Jesus said to a man, "'Follow Me.' But the man replied, 'Lord, first let me go and bury my father.' Jesus said to him, 'Let the dead bury their own dead, but you go and proclaim the kingdom of God'" (Luke 9:59,60).

Jesus also said "Blessed are the poor in spirit, for theirs is the kingdom of heaven" (Matt. 5:33). Perhaps He was really meaning, "Blessed are the uncluttered in spirit!"

SEEKING FIRST THE KINGDOM IS BEING AMBITIOUS FOR GOD'S PURPOSES

William Booth was the cofounder of the Salvation Army. One of his biographers tells of a day when General Booth, who was at that time in his 80s, was ill and had been to see a physician. The doctor charged Booth's son, Bramwell, with the task of telling his dad that he would soon be losing his eyesight. "You mean that I am going blind?" "Well, General, I fear that we must contemplate that," said Bramwell, who along with the other family members had always addressed their father by that affectionate name. Booth paused a while to consider what he had been told. Then the General asked, "I shall never see your face again?" "No, probably not in this world," was the son's reply. The biographer writes, "During the next few moments the veteran's hands crept along the counterpane to take hold of his son's; holding it, he very calmly responded, 'God must know best!' Then, after another pause, 'Bramwell, I have done what I could for God and for the people with my eyes. Now I shall do what I can for God and for the people without my eyes.'"[4]

General Booth modeled the words of Paul in Acts 20:24:

> But none of these things move me; nor do I count my life dear to myself, so that I may finish my race with joy, and the ministry which I received from the Lord Jesus, to testify to the gospel of the grace of God.

When we choose to lay selfishness aside, we are bound to encounter an inner battle, but we must persevere if we desire to be profitable for the kingdom of God. To be ambitious for God's purposes means that we prioritize our schedules around things that are of eternal consequence. And in our emotional makeup, we devote our passions and feelings to representing God well in our homes, schools, businesses and churches. We don't *spend* our time; we *invest* it in creating a life that is well pleasing to the Lord. In so doing, we protect our passions and energies to ensure that God is first and glorified in all that we think, say and do.

SEEKING FIRST THE KINGDOM IS GIVING GOD THE PRIORITY DUE HIM

Jesus is the Good Shepherd (see John 10:14). Just as the modern-day shepherd knows each trail and each sheep by name, so Jesus is our Good Shepherd who knows you and me by our names and knows the path that each one of us should take. As we seek God first and give Him priority in our lives, Jesus becomes not only our Good Shepherd but also our Master, our Manager and our Owner.

Typically, a shepherd will put his mark on his sheep. Some shepherds use their knives to notch one ear of each of their sheep. Though painful, the notch signifies a mark of ownership. Similarly, as we give God priority in our lives, He will use the painful things in our experiences as marks of ownership that identify us with Him. Then, with the Chief Shepherd directing our paths, our wills begin to flow in concert with His. Our words echo those of the apostle Paul:

> Brethren, I do not count myself to have apprehended; but one thing I do, forgetting those things which are behind and reaching forward to those things which are ahead, I press toward the goal for the prize of the upward call of God in Christ Jesus (Phil. 3:13,14).

When our lives are aligned with the Kingdom, we are no longer exploited by society's expectation that we should be too busy and too overworked to do anything else. We refuse the lie that says we must be busy in order to be important. When God is our priority, we cannot be intoxicated by the drivenness that accompanies an overloaded lifestyle. We understand that "in quietness and confidence shall be your strength" (Isa. 30:15).

America claims to be a Judeo-Christian nation. We have imprinted "IN GOD WE TRUST" upon our currency; however, most people—even

"When God is our priority, we cannot be intoxicated by the drivenness that accompanies an overloaded lifestyle"

Christians—trust more in their money and what it can buy than they do in God. Who is rearranging Christian values? What will you do to make God a priority in your home, your city, your state? The main thing is to keep the main thing the main thing. The main thing is to make Jesus the Lord—to give God the priority due Him.

SEEKING FIRST THE KINGDOM IS SEEKING HIS RULE, HIS WILL, HIS AUTHORITY

When we become true believers in Jesus Christ, we have moved out of one kingdom and into another. Colossians 1:13,14 explains:

> He has delivered us from the power of darkness and conveyed us into the kingdom of the Son of His love, in whom we have redemption through His blood, the forgiveness of sins.

According to this biblical passage from Colossians, we were under the rule, will and authority of the king of darkness, the devil, but now we are to be under the rule, will and authority of the Lord Jesus, transported into the kingdom of God. And we come under the rule and authority of Christ by seeking God first in every decision. As we seek obedience to God's kingdom, the parts of our lives that have been damaged through sin are restored.

But God's arch enemy, Satan, cannot stand to see God's children blessed. He knows that the way to hurt God is to hurt His children. Therefore, the enemy comes to steal, kill and destroy them. But he can only do so successfully if we do not place our lives constantly under the immediate rule and authority of the Lord Jesus.

We fail, we fall, we stumble. The same old flaws and failures seek to pursue us throughout our lifetimes. We can blame bad genes, dysfunctional families, demented ancestors or even demons—and those things can influence our lives, but usually we are our own worst enemies. We sabotage the good that God has for us by removing ourselves from His rule. Most of us want to conquer the sins that "so easily entangle us" (Heb. 12:1). Therefore, the quicker we come under the power and authority of the Lord Jesus, the more quickly we will see those things fall off so that God restore us to the place where He can use us.

We can walk in alignment with God if we will just apply the message of the following song to our lives:

Trust and obey
> For there is no other way
> > To be happy in Jesus
> > > Than to trust and obey.

SEEKING FIRST THE KINGDOM IS SUBMITTING COMPLETELY TO THE HOLY SPIRIT

Living in complete submission to the Holy Spirit means receiving a new heart and allowing Christ to dwell in that heart. Ezekiel 36:26,27 says, "I will give you a new heart and put a new spirit within you. I will take the heart of stone out of your flesh and give you a heart of flesh. I will put my spirit within you and cause you to walk in my statutes and you will keep my judgments and do them."

The work of the Holy Spirit begins when He is welcomed into your heart. That work is advanced when He is permitted full reign. When we allow sin to rule or reign in our lives, our conscience is weakened and we refuse to submit ourselves to the Holy Spirit. Believers make many decisions outside of the blessing of God that result in sinful behavior and rebellious attitudes. Thus, seeking first the Kingdom is sensitizing our hearts to anything that offends God:

Ephesians 4:30: Do not grieve the Holy Spirit of God, by whom you were sealed for the day of redemption.

Hebrews 10:22: Let us draw near with a true heart with full assurance of faith, having our hearts sprinkled from an evil conscience and our bodies washed with pure water.

God has given each one of us a natural facility called "the conscience" that acts like an inner umpire or a warning signal to let us know when we are outside of God's supernatural call on our lives. But if we refuse to give heed to those warnings, our consciences will cease to protect us. Those who have extinguished their consciences begin, "speaking lies in hypocrisy, having their own conscience *seared* with a hot iron" (1 Tim. 4:2, emphasis added).

The word "seared" in the Greek means to be withered, dried up, inactive; it indicates a conscience that is insensitive to sin. With repeated abuse and unrepented sin, the conscience is nullified; it falls silent and leaves the person flying blindly through life. And even though the warning signals are gone, the danger certainly is not. In fact, the danger becomes far greater.

The kingdom of evil has declared war on guilt, presenting the concept as medieval, obsolete and nonproductive. But if our adversary cannot convince us that we have nothing to feel guilty about, he will use condemnation and shame to cause us to run way from God. The result is that multitudes of people, including believers, respond to their consciences by attempting to suppress, overrule or silence them. We blame our actions on someone else, or deny any guilt at all by attempting to hide the evidence. At times we try to punish ourselves as a means of serving time for bad behavior. We can even rationalize sin, making excuses by justifying the circumstances. The problem is that when we seek to handle guilt on our own terms, it doesn't go away—it merely roots itself more deeply in the soil of our lives.

The only way to uproot, or remove, guilt is to first repent of it—which means that you acknowledge what you did as being rebellious toward God, you agree with God that it was wrong and you accept responsibility for changing your future actions. Second, you cover your sin with the shed blood of the Lord Jesus—which means that you accept God's forgiveness and that you forgive yourself. Then, you will find that God can plant something new where the sin once took hold.

People who live in Kingdom alignment are sensitive to sin and anything that offends God, because love for God is the driving force of their lives. They are transparent before God and quick to respond to the conviction of the Holy Spirit so that He can weed out the things that could weaken them for Kingdom purposes. Listen to the way Porter Barrington, Editor of *The Christian Life New Testament*, has so eloquently described a life that is submitted to the Holy Spirit:

"The fruit of the Spirit is love," and it is manifested in:

1. Joy, which is love's strength.

2. Peace, which is love's security.

3. Long-suffering, which is love's patience.

4. Gentleness, which is love's conduct.

5. Goodness, which is love's character.

6. Faith, which is love's confidence.

7. Meekness, which is love's humility.

8. Temperance, which is love's victory.

"Against such there is no law."

A Holy-Spirit-controlled person needs no law to cause him or her to live a righteous life. The secret of a Spirit-controlled life is found in dedication to God. Put your all on the altar, and the Holy Spirit will fill your heart with the love of God.[5]

In other words, "Seek first the kingdom of God and His righteousness, and all these things shall be added to you" (Matt. 6:33).

NOTES

1   Rob Gilbert, ed., *Bits & Pieces* (Fairfield, N.J.: The Economics Press, December 30, 1999), p. 16.

2   Dr. and Mrs. Howard Taylor, *Hudson Taylor's Spiritual Secret* (Chicago, Moody Press, 1987), pp. 19-20.

3   Charles R. Swindoll, *The Tale of the Tardy Oxcart* (Nashville: Word Publishing, 1998), p. 308.

4   Gordon MacDonald, *The Life That God Blesses* (Nashville: Thomas Nelson Publishers, 1994), pp. 65-66.

5   Porter Barrington, ed., *The Christian Life New Testament With the Psalms* (Nashville: Thomas Nelson Publishers, 1978), p. 342, adapted.

First Remove the Log from Your Own Eye

Aligning Your Attitudes

"First get rid of the log from your own eye; then perhaps you will see well enough to deal with the speck in your friend's eye."
—Matthew 7:5 (NLT)

Two taxidermists stopped before a window in which an owl was on display. They immediately began to criticize the way the owl was mounted. Its eyes were not natural; its wings were not in proportion with its head; its feathers were not neatly arranged; and its feet needed improvement. When they finally exhausted their list of criticisms, the old owl turned its head and winked at them.

Perhaps it was that wise old owl who said, "The art of being wise is the art of knowing what to overlook." We can all be criticized for something, but our criticism says a lot more about us than it does about those we are judging. Listen to the words of Jesus in Matthew 7:1-5 from *The Message*:

"Don't pick on people, jump on their failure, criticize their faults—unless you want the same treatment. That critical spirit has a way of boomeranging. It's easy to see a smudge on your neighbor's face and be oblivious to the sneer on your own. Do you have the nerve to say, 'Let me wash your face for you,' when your own face is distorted by contempt? It's this whole traveling-road-show mentality all over again, playing a holier-than-thou part instead of just living your part. Wipe that ugly sneer off your own face, and you might be fit to offer a washcloth to your neighbor."

Criticizing and judging others is a sin that most of us struggle with, at least occasionally, so let us be open to what the Holy Spirit has to say on this subject.

There's Hope for the Judgmental

Few people have finished their race in life without judging someone for something; far too many, however, have charged through life's corridors judging almost everyone for something. These discontented souls have a deep-rooted fault-finding flaw that is obvious to others but rarely ever acknowledged in themselves. For those with a nagging bent toward this trait, judging may have been so generationally seeded in their family systems that "the fruit hasn't fallen far from the tree." Perhaps judgmentalism is a flaw that has permeated your family's roots. Don't worry, the good news is that there is hope for all of us to overcome the vile tendency of judging others—and that hope is in Christ.

Jesus' words recorded about the speck and the log from Matthew 7:5 say that I will mirror my judgments of others because I will find in myself what I look for in others. As Christians, you and I are to mirror Jesus and judge ourselves so that we don't have to be judged by the Holy Spirit. We are to be going from glory to glory (see 2 Cor. 3:18)—and we do that by focusing on Jesus, not other people.

Fortunately, no matter where we are spiritually, the greatest hope of the gospel is set in 2 Corinthians 5:17 and Ephesians 2:17. These biblical passages assure us that we can be changed; we can become new creatures in Christ. No character flaw or problem has so fully ravaged our souls that the Holy Spirit cannot redeem and, through that redemptive process, bring in a new character strength.

SMALL FLAWS CAN PRODUCE BIG PROBLEMS

On January 28, 1986, a tiny flaw caused a tragic accident. Seven astronauts boarded Space Shuttle Challenger headed for the space station. Suddenly, a flaw in a small rubber ring caused a small leak, which caused a small flame, which led to a massive explosion that destroyed the shuttle and killed all those aboard. Similarly, a small flaw in our character can launch a massive destructive force in our lives. It is our responsibility, therefore, to stay watchful for character defects that have the power to undermine our callings.

Second Corinthians 5:17 says that "if anyone is in Christ, he is a new creation; old things have passed away; behold, all things have become new." During the course of this chapter, would you please pray this Scripture. I'm concerned that some of the following material could be convicting, and I want you to be reminded of the promise in this verse, which says that God can and will change you, if you will live in Him and obey His Word.

JUDGING VERSUS DISCERNMENT

Jesus says in Matthew 7:1-5, "Judge not, that you be not judged. For with what judgment you judge, you will be judged; and with the measure you use, it will be measured back to you. And why do you look at the speck in your brother's eye, but do not consider the plank in your own eye? Or how can you say to your brother, 'Let me remove the speck from your eye'; and look, a plank is in your own eye? Hypocrite! First remove the plank from your own eye, and then you will see clearly to remove the speck out of your brother's eye."

The Lord begins by exhorting us not to pass judgment on others. But what does Jesus mean when He tells us not to judge? Does He mean that all manner of judgment is absolutely and without qualification forbidden so that with respect to our neighbors, we are not allowed to form and/or express any opinions whatsoever? Does He mean that we must never voice an adverse or unfavorable opinion? No way! Jesus Himself said, "Do not judge according to appearance, but [do] judge with righteous judgment" (John 7:24). He also said, "You will know [or judge] them by their fruits" (Matt. 7:16). In light of what Jesus said throughout the Scriptures, we must even judge and regard certain individuals as being dogs and hogs (see Matt. 7:6; 1 Cor. 5:12; 6:1-5; Gal. 1:8,9, Phil. 3:2; 1 John 4:1).

> "Only by listening to the Holy Spirit can we discern between the hurting people we are to help and the hurting people that will malign our Kingdom purposes."

Only by listening to the Holy Spirit can we discern between the hurting people we are to help and the hurting people that will malign our Kingdom purposes. No one can be all things to all people; however, when each member of the body acts out of obedience to God, the Church becomes heaven's tool for solving earthly problems.

For example, a woman in our congregation sensed a God-given burden for the hurting street kids here in Portland. She realized that she couldn't tell of God's love unless she first *showed* it, so she became the City Bible Church Cookie Monster! She started baking cookies and using the cookies as a foundation for building trust with this younger generation. Eventually, one of the youths was killed, and this dear woman wrapped the arms of Jesus around the kids by providing the funeral. Today, a bunch of those same kids are members of our church family.

A word of caution: When you and I discern who are the people God wants us to minister to, we can slip into the lamentable mind-set of thinking that everyone should echo our call to that mission. Beware! Such erroneous thinking can spawn attitudes of judgment toward other believers and toward the church.

Another warning for those who minister to hurting people: Don't reverse the counseling roles! Permit me to explain. My wife, Sharon, and I often try to relate to our unsave friends and neighbors—and some of those people espouse quite deviant lifestyles. However, though we allow unbelievers to come into our home, we do not permit them to give us or our children advice or influence our family in any way. We believe that God has called us to change the worldly by respecting their personhood without endorsing their lifestyles.

Respect for others is an indication of self-respect. By recognizing and accepting the limitations of your own nature, you can be more considerate and understanding of others. To build the community of the Kingdom, Jesus asked the disciples to avoid a judgmental attitude, to avoid prejudgment or prejudice, to refrain from stereotyping others because doing so would limit their possibilities for fulfillment. The old adage that says, "Do not judge your neighbor until you have walked in his shoes" is somewhat a valid statement, but we all wear out our soles differently!

If you attempt to walk in someone else's shoes, you may trip over your own ego. After all, judgmentalism is just an ego trip (pun intended). We usually judge to make ourselves feel better; and yet, what really happens is that our judgments almost always boomerang. A judgmental attitude estranges us from others, hinders our spirit of fellowship and creates a reaction of judgment in return. Thus, judgment causes us to feel worse about ourselves rather than better.

WHY WE OUGHT NOT TO JUDGE

The reasons for withholding our judgments of others are many, but in this chapter we will simply consider three. First, we only know in part, never fully understanding all the issues or motives behind another person's actions. Second, we are incapable of being completely impartial because we have unconscious emotions that affect our judgments, causing us to critique others based on feelings rather than truth. Third, only God, in His holiness and understanding, is competent to judge another. James writes, "Who are you to judge another?" (Jas. 4:12).

Conversely, Matthew 7:5 does not allow us to escape the discernment that will help another. We are first to judge ourselves and find the correction that God's grace can achieve. Then, when our heart's are aligned with the Father's heart, we will be able to take the speck out of our brother's eye. Refusing to be judgmental does not mean that we refuse to be helpful. Helping your brother or sister at his or her point of need can mean telling the truth in love, which is discerning the problem and becoming part of the solution.

It's not unusual to hear Christians use their fear of being judgmental as an excuse for laxity in exercising church discipline. But Scripture tells us that "if a man is overtaken in any trespass, you who are spiritual restore such a one in a spirit of gentleness, considering yourself lest you also be tempted" (Gal. 6:1). Additionally, we are given a specific order for carrying out church discipline:

> "Moreover if your brother sins against you, go and tell him his fault between you and him alone. If he hears you, you have gained your brother. But if he will not hear, take with you one or two more, that 'by the mouth of two or three witnesses every word may be established.' And if he refuses to hear them, tell it to the church. But if he refuses even to hear the church, let him be to you like a heathen and a tax collector" (Matt. 18:15-17).

God has offered this method of church discipline in order to protect the innocent. He never tells us to be critics for the sheer pleasure of putting others down. We are all accountable to each other (see 1 Pet. 5:5).

Notice that we must first judge ourselves and take inventory of our own lives (see Matt. 7:3-5). We are not called to police each other's personalities; we are called to police our own personalities. When we try to reposition the Holy Spirit in others' lives so that we can gain control, we risk wounding the Body of Christ and grieving the heart of God. How will you know whether you are guilty? As someone has said, "If one person calls you a donkey, forget it. However, if several people have called you a donkey, go buy a saddle!"

One way that we can determine if we're in the market for a saddle is by listening to our judgments of others—it takes one to know one! The Pharisees had an innate propensity for severely condemning others while making excuses for their own faults—and we Christians are not exempt from being guilty of the same inclination (see Rom. 2:1). Jesus condemns anyone who would judge another harshly or unmercifully while overlooking his or her own need for change.

HOPE FOR HYPERCRITICAL FAULTFINDERS

Yes, both discrimination and criticism can sometimes be necessary, but there is no excuse for being hypercritical. We should avoid saying what is untrue (see Exod. 23:1), unnecessary (see Prov. 11:13) and unkind (see Prov. 18:8). People walking in Kingdom alignment understand that criticism ought to be sandwiched between two large slices of praise in order to build up the other members of the Body—but hypercritical faultfinders are all about tearing people down. They are the self-appointed judges of the world; they're nit-picky, critical, harsh, petty, overly strict, severe, rigid, demanding and hard-to-live-with kinds of people. They themselves are overly sensitive to criticism and yet their criticism toward others is biting. They use their moods to manipulate others, and most of them would rather be right than be happy. Above all, they are incapable of admitting when they are wrong.

Let me ask you some introspective questions:

- Do you find it easier to see what is wrong with others than you do to zoom in on what is right with them?
- Do most of your criticisms humiliate rather than edify the other person?
- Do you insist on being right, rather than righting your wrongs?
- Do you resist asking for forgiveness when you discover that you were at fault?
- Do you think that being cynical is normal?
- Do you believe that sarcasm is a social grace—one that actually causes people to like you more?

If you answered yes to any of these questions, it's time to confront and rid yourself of a faultfinding attitude. Faultfinding is a character flaw that emotionally wounds and devastates people, even those closest to you—and sometimes even without your knowing it. Faultfinding can also be a defense mechanism: you quickly judge others before they have the opportunity to judge you. Let's take a moment to pray about this problem:

Dear heavenly Father,
I confess to You that I have allowed the habit of faultfinding to take root in me. I ask that You weed this ungodly attitude out of my life and seed me with a desire to see the best in myself and others. Please forgive me for being so prideful. Please show me how I have hurt others and grace me with the courage to make amends. Your Word says that if we confess our sins, You are faithful and just to forgive us—so I receive Your forgiveness right now. Thank You for loving me; please show me how to truly love others. In Jesus' name I pray. Amen.

THE THINKING BEHIND A
NEGATIVE MENTAL ATTITUDE

Now that we have asked the Lord to forgive us for judging others, let's make sure that we stay on alert for negative mental attitudes. The following are some of the erroneous things we begin to believe before we fall into the trap of negativity and faultfinding:

1. *I see things as they really are.* Now ask yourself: Am I seeing things as God sees them? Am I erring on the side of pessimism and losing the hope of God in this situation?

2. *Life is unfair.* Ask yourself: Is there anything about my situation that I can take responsibility for changing? Am I where I'm at because life is unfair, or are there some attitudes I need to change?

3. *Life owes me a better way, but there is none.* Ask yourself: Does anybody really owe me anything? I may have had a bad childhood or some bad breaks in life, but what have I done to make it better?

4. *Life is filled with problems that have no solutions.* Ask yourself: Would the most successful person I know be able to solve this problem? Am I willing to humble myself and ask for help?

5. *It's dangerous to be happy.* Ask yourself: Do I really want to be happy, or would I rather have people feel sorry for me? If I were to be happy, what would I have to change about me?

6. *God can't; and if He could, He wouldn't.* Ask yourself: What's greater—God or my problem? Am I telling the truth about God's character based on His Word?

When we cultivate judgmental attitudes, we lose our virtue. We turn our backs on the goodness of God. Jesus is the Restorer, not the destroyer. We know who the destroyer is—he is the devil. John 10:10 says that the devil comes to steal, kill and destroy. Thus, when we allow judgmental attitudes to permeate our souls, we invite the destroyer to have his way in our lives.

TAMING THE PESSIMISTICALLY CHALLENGED TONGUE

Art Linkletter said that "things usually turn out best for those who make the best of the way that things turn out." But some people don't seem to want to find a way out of their problems. They would rather bemoan the cause for their problems—"Life is unfair because. . .Life owes me because. . .I can't change because. . ."—than they would take responsibility for changing. When Jesus encountered these kinds of people, His question was always the same: Do you want to be healed?

A story is told of twins who were raised by an abusive, alcoholic father. The older of the two grew up and became not only a loving father and husband but also the mayor of his town. The younger of the twins became an angry drunk, who spent much of his life disturbing the peace and serving time in jail. One day a reporter came to town to interview the two men. When the reporter asked the men why each one had become who he was, both men replied, "My father." The older twin insisted that because he had not judged his father, he was able to use his father's mistakes to keep him out of trouble. The younger twin insisted that because his father had been such a cruel and angry man, he was doomed to repeating his father's mistakes. The bottom line is that our choice in attitude always matters. The way I see it, one man wanted to be healed; the other was too comfortable bathing in a pool of self-pity!

> "When we hide behind the ebonic veil of pessimism, saying that our circumstances cannot be changed because our lives are the blame of someone else's actions, we make the choice to drink the poison of self-pity."

When we hide behind the ebonic veil of pessimism, saying that our circumstances cannot be changed because our lives are the blame of someone else's actions, we make the choice to drink the poison of self-pity. Our tongues then become rabid, striking out at those who have what we don't have—even though the elusiveness of what we want is due to our own choices.

Perhaps Linkletter was right: Things will turn out best for those who make the best of the way things turn out. We're all going to encounter problems, but we can chose to become either bitter or better because of them.

Cynicism is a sign that we have turned away from trusting God and instead chosen to trust in the flesh, our carnal nature. Those who trust God are able to say like the apostle Paul:

> But we have this treasure in earthen vessels, that the excellence of the power may be of God and not of us. We are hard pressed on every side, yet not crushed; we are perplexed, but not in despair; persecuted, but not forsaken; struck down, but not destroyed (2 Cor. 4:7-9).

James said that you and I should "count it all joy when you fall into various trials" (Jas. 1:2). Notice the word "when." We can all expect to encounter problems, but our solutions are found in faith in Christ and God's written Word. The same Word that created the heavens and the earth is the same Word that can speak into your situation and change everything. God's Word is always greater than the words of your enemy.

Judgmental people, however, are afraid to trust God. They live in the fear realm rather than the faith realm. And because they've been disappointed in the past, they fear that they will be disappointed in the future. By refusing to hope in God, they are actually judging Him—which is obviously a huge character flaw and a horrible way to live. Because they are afraid to allow themselves to be happy, they allow their unhappiness to leech the happiness out of others' lives. My question to those people is, If it is dangerous for you yourself to be happy and fulfilled, how can you ever be positive toward anyone else who is happy and fulfilled?

Thankfully, the pessimistically challenged tongue can be changed. To begin to change the tongue, your attitude must change. To change your attitude, your heart must change. To change your heart, your belief in the Lord Jesus Christ and the Holy Spirit must change. And to change your beliefs about Him, the Word of God must be planted in your heart so that your confessions change. Romans 10:17 puts is this way: So then faith comes by hearing, and hearing by the word of God.

DEVELOPING A POSITIVE
ATTITUDE TOWARD OTHERS

Instead of nurturing judgmental attitudes, we can and should develop a positive attitude toward others. But in order to change our negative attitudes, we have to change our thinking. Philippians 4:8 says, "Finally, brethren, whatever things are true, whatever things are noble, whatever things are just, whatever things are pure, whatever things are lovely, whatever things are of good report, if there is any virtue and if there is anything praiseworthy—meditate on these things." Why not write a list of things that you can begin to meditate on immediately which would change the way you think and speak. To think on things that are lovely and of good report means that you surround yourself with and build an atmosphere of lovely things and things that are of good report, things that are praiseworthy. That might even mean changing some of your relationships.

How about changing your outlook on life? Philippians 4:13 is a great confession and a great way to start. It says that "I can do all things through Christ who strengthens me." In other words, with God's help, I can even change the way I see others and the way I look at life.

YOU CAN

You can change your outlook on life. Oh yes you can. All you need to do is replace the words "I can't" with "I can." The "can'ts" must go, because with a Spirit-led ability to see what God wants done, you have the power to do whatever He asks. When your life is aligned with the Holy Spirit, you will have total faith, trust, confidence and certainty that God will accomplish whatever He chooses to do in your life.

Another translation (TCNT) of Philippians 4:13 reads, "Nothing is beyond my power and the strength of Him who makes me strong, I am ready for anything through the strength of him who is working in me."

The following are 10 good confessions for a person desiring to change his or her outlook on life:

Yes. . .I can Believe (see Mark 9:24; Heb. 11:6; Jas. 2:19).

Yes. . .I can Change (see 2 Cor. 3:18; Rom. 12:1).

Yes. . .I can Love and be Loved (see John 13:34; Rom. 5:5; Eph. 5:2).

Yes. . .I can Forgive and be Forgiven (see Eph. 4:32; 1 John 2:12).

Yes. . .I can Rule my Thought Life (see 2 Cor. 10:2,3; Phil. 4:7,8).

Yes. . .I can Make a Difference (see Esther 4:14; Acts 13:36).

Yes. . .I can Accomplish Great Things (see Hab. 2:1-4; John 14:12).

Yes. . .I can Stand in the midst of Adverse Circumstances
    (see 2 Sam. 23:11,12; Eph. 6:13,14).

Yes. . .I can Defeat the Enemy (see Rom. 8:31,37; 1 John 4:4).

Yes. . .I can Be a Finisher (see 2 Tim. 4:6,7).

Let us make a commitment to ourselves and to the Lord that we will allow the Holy Spirit to change us. None of us really wants to be faultfinders, cynical or negative. We want to be known as positive people with a positive outlook and a Christlike nature.

Henry David Thoreau said, "The faultfinder will find fault even in paradise." But we can make a commitment to first remove the beam from our own eyes so that we can see the attributes of paradise in others. Will you join me in making a decision to change the way you see, think and talk about people? Ask the Holy Spirit for a new set of Kingdom glasses so that your vision is aligned with your heavenly Father's. If you do, you will discover that believing is seeing–and in seeing, you won't find more than a speck in your brother's eye.

First Be Reconciled To Your Brother
Aligning Your Relationships

"First be reconciled to your brother, and then come and offer your gift."
—Matthew 5:23

A Roman emperor sought to discover humanity's original language—thinking it might be Hebrew, Greek or Latin. So he experimented by isolating a few infants. The nurses involved were sworn to absolute silence, and no one ever spoke to or in the presence of the children. The babies heard not a word, not a single sound from a human voice. Tragically, within several months, they all died. A lamentable result of a bizarre search for knowledge gone awry, the emperor never learned the original language of humankind—but he did prove one thing: people cannot survive without relationships.[1]

Relationships with God and others are key to the meaning of life; they define who we are. Therefore, if we want to walk in Kingdom alignment, we must discover God's will for our relationships. We were created for God and for each other; that is why every generation hungers for a relational place to belong, a place to call home. But twenty-first-century people seem to be facing an unprecedented loss of relational cohesion.

Many of us are endeavoring to build or rebuild relationships without the skills and the knowledge to do so. And because the dysfunctional family does not provide the community that it was designed to offer, the local church must become a healthy place where relationships can be built in a trusting, loving community.

When Jesus came to earth, He laid the foundation for repairing relationships. Let's read Matthew 5:23-25 together:

> "Therefore if you bring your gift to the altar, and there remember that your brother has something against you, leave your gift there before the altar, and go your way. First be reconciled to your brother, and then come and offer your gift. Agree with your adversary quickly, while you are on the way with him, lest your adversary deliver you to the judge, the judge hand you over to the officer, and you be thrown into prison."

As the Church, the family of God, our goal is to help people build new relationships, restore old relationships, renew some neglected relationships and commit to cultivating authentic relationships. We believe every home should create an atmosphere where love, acceptance and connecting with people flows naturally, so the local church should establish an example for unsaved families to follow. The church atmosphere should be one of authentic, biblical *koinonia*, where people are relating one to another easily and honestly. Jesus applies the law of firsts to relationships by teaching that relationships come before ministry or gifts or accomplishments. They are to be first in time and value.

REPAIRING RELATIONSHIPS

In Matthew 5:23, the Lord explains the importance of understanding that during our lifetimes, we will have ample opportunities to practice reconciling with our brothers and sisters. In other words, we won't run out of chances for learning how to make peace with those whom God has joined to us. We should continually be attempting to gain understanding of others so that we can build bridges of relational connection rather than walls that block people out of our lives.

When asked on his deathbed by his priest if he would forgive all his enemies, the Spanish General Rom·n Maria Narv·ez growled, "I do not have to forgive my enemies. I have had them all shot!"[2] As believers, we are to forgive our enemies, forgive our friends, forgive anyone who has trespassed against us, and ask forgiveness of those whom we have trespassed against.

Listen to the way Matthew 5:23 is translated in the *Amplified Bible*:

"Leave your gift at the altar and go. First make peace with your brother and then come back and present your gift. Come to terms quickly with your accuser while you are on the way traveling with him, lest your accuser hand you over to the judge, and the judge to the guard and you be put in prison."

Our responsibility is to build relationships; and if they get damaged, to know how to repair them, restoring them to perfect health. One of our first steps in the Christian life should be toward first reconciling with those we have anything against. But "a brother offended is harder to win than a strong city, and contentions are like the bars of a castle" (Prov. 18:19). Of course, we've probably all learned through personal experience that reconciliation is hard work—it's emotionally, mentally and spiritually trying. But it is usually possible.

If reconciliation is a harder battle to win than conquering a strong city, it's no wonder that we usually put off confrontations, ultimately forgetting about them in hopes that they will simply disappear forever. Many of us have cruised through life wanting to build permanent new relationships upon the soggy seas of past relational failures. And though the wake that follows us billows with waves of unsettled matter, we keep hoping to anchor in a harbor of carefree relational bliss. We want to moor in a place with no need for forgiveness or reconciliation or pressure of any kind. How unrealistic! All relationships—whether they are with immediate family, close friends, coworkers or acquaintances—need routine maintenance and occasional repair in order to function well.

UNHEALTHY INDIVIDUALISM

One thing that seeks to sabotage our need for relational intimacy is unhealthy individualism. "Individualism lies at the very core of American culture. We believe in the dignity, indeed even the sacredness of the individual. Anything that would violate our right to think for ourselves, judge for ourselves, make our own decisions, live our lives as we see fit is not only morally wrong but it is also sacrilegious. As much as we want community, we shy away whenever it infringes on our autonomy!"[3]

Fear of rejection, fear of embarrassment or fear of simply not knowing how to handle intimacy can cause us to back off from others and live in isolation. But isolation is not the will of God, and it is not how the kingdom of God functions.

Most of us are working too many hours and often both spouses are working. With school activities, community activities and church activities, the pace of society seems to be accelerating. Exhaustive busyness and fears have hindered our ability to develop intimate, lasting relationships. It's time to face this dilemma and deal with it. We can begin by making relationships top priority in our schedules. The more time we invest in nurturing our relationships, the less time we will have to spend in repairing them.

THE DECISION TO FORGIVE

In *The Message*, Eugene Peterson translates Matthew 5:23-25 as follows:

"This is how I want you to conduct yourself in these matters. If you enter your place of worship and, about to make an offering, you suddenly remember a grudge a friend has against you, abandon your offering, leave immediately, go to this friend and make things right. Then and only then, come back and work things out with God. Or say you're out on the street and an old enemy accosts you. Don't lose a minute. Make the first move; make things right with him. After all, if you leave the first move to him, knowing his track record, you're likely to end up in court, maybe even in jail. If that happens, you won't get out without a stiff fine."

Forgiveness is a willful decision—and not an easy one. Most of us wait for the other person to say something, do something or show that he or she is open to speaking with us before we seek any resolve. Jesus rightly says in effect, "First above all else, first in time and right, first in importance, you are to make up your mind that you will make the first move in repairing relationships and be a true reconciler of the brethren."

I heard an unforgettable story about forgiveness from the Truth and Reconciliation Commission that granted whole or partial amnesty to perpetrators of violence in the old South Africa of racial apartheid. The amnesty was given in exchange for the truth; perpetrators had to tell their crimes with the victims in the room. One of those victims was an elderly black woman who stood in that South African courtroom, facing a man who seemingly did not desire to be forgiven. Mr. Van der Broek, a white security police officer, had been found guilty of murdering the woman's only son as well as her husband.

Van der Broek had come to the woman's home years earlier, taken her son and shot him at point-blank range, then burned his body while he and some other officers reveled in their act. Several years later, Van der Broek returned to take her husband as well. For two years, this wife could learn nothing of her beloved husband's whereabouts. Then, Van der Broek came back for the woman herself. She was led to a place beside a river. There, she saw her husband bound and beaten, lying on a pile of wood. As the officers poured gasoline over his body and set him aflame, his last words were, "Father, forgive them."

But justice caught up with Mr. Van der Broek. He'd been found guilty, and it was time to determine his fate. The presiding official of the court asked the woman, "So what do you want? How should justice be meted out to this man who has so brutally destroyed your family?"

The woman responded, "I want three things. I want first to be taken to the place where my husband's body was burned so I can gather up the dust and give his remains a decent burial." She paused, then continued. "My husband and my son were my only family. Therefore, second,

I want Mr. Van der Broek to become my son. I want him to come twice a month to the ghetto and spend a day with me so that I can pour out on him whatever love I still have remaining within me. And finally, I want a third thing. I would like Mr. Van der Broek to know that I offer him my forgiveness because Jesus Christ died to forgive. This was also the wish of my husband. And so, I would kindly ask someone to come to my side and lead me across the courtroom so that I can take Mr. Van der Broek in my arms, embrace him and let him know that he is truly forgiven." 4

What a contrast! A bitter general who shot his enemies and an elderly woman who understood the grace of God, making reconciliation a first in her life and loving her enemy as a son.

KINGDOM FOCUS, THE REASON FOR FORGIVENESS

> "Forgiveness is what we do to clean out our hearts so that Jesus Christ can occupy His rightful place there."

Of course, in telling the story of this South African woman, I do not want to imply that anyone should return to an abusive or evil relationship. Kingdom focus is the reason for forgiving. None of us can focus on two things at once. Therefore, when our lives are full of unforgiveness, we focus on the person who hurt us rather than on the person of Jesus Christ. Forgiveness is what we do to clean out our hearts so that Jesus Christ can occupy His rightful place there. Permit me to explain through an illustration in my own life.

I first became acquainted with the concept of Kingdom focus at Bill Gothard's Basic Youth Conflicts seminar many years ago. At that time, I was struggling so much with hurt over my relationship with my father that I couldn't seem to move out into all that I knew God had for me. My dad had been both a pastor and the father of seven children, but it seemed to me that he was so busy helping everyone else that I became insignificant. I had judged my dad for not meeting my expectations, and that judgment was hindering my relationship with God and others.

So after the seminar, I wrote my father a long letter, asking him to forgive me for judging him and telling him how much I desired a right relationship with him. That letter was just what Doctor Jesus prescribed to heal my heart and my spiritual sight. I'll never forget the release I experienced when I realized that by forgiving my father and putting the focus back on the Lord Jesus, I was finally free to be the person God wanted me to become.

You might need to forgive someone who is deceased, dangerous or unavailable. In anyone of these cases, let the act of forgiving be between you and the Lord.

PACIFISM IS NOT THE ANSWER

In lieu of the atrocity that occurred in New York City on September 11, 2001, I want you to understand that when I talk about forgiveness in this chapter, I recognize that we are in a battle against evil. I would never use forgiveness as an excuse for the cowardly, immoral pacifism that does not seek to stop evil men who wreak terror against the innocent and the weak. I recognize that love is about protection.

I also recognize that pacifism seeks to impose its Lilly-livered, naive and narcissistic "moral superiority" on a gullible public. And yet, it only succeeds in aiding and abetting violent men. So please know that at no time am I suggesting that we protect evil by pursuing forgiveness.
With that said, let's focus on how forgiveness can change the relationships that we do want to maintain.

THREE ASPECTS OF RELATIONSHIP

Because sin seeks to twist the reality of healthy interpersonal relationships, leaving people hungering for the realization of relational dreams, the only true relational dream that we can aspire to is the one Jesus paints for us in the Bible. That is, we, who are born of this earth, need to be born again so that we have a new nature, a nature consistent with the image of God's Son, the Lord Jesus Christ. Our new nature affords us the ability to draw from the Holy Spirit within us those

41

things that are needful for building good relationships and repairing broken ones. Our dreams can only be realized within Kingdom alignment.

For now, we will consider three general categories of Kingdom relationships:

1. biblical fellowship, or acquaintances
2. Kingdom partnerships, or fellow workers
3. covenant relationships, or intimate friendships

Generally speaking, all Christians in America have access to biblical fellowship—the community of God's people. We also have a responsibility to develop Kingdom partnerships as we work together in accomplishing the purposes of God. And then, every single one of us needs and desires close friendships—what I call "covenant relationships."

BIBLICAL FELLOWSHIP

The word "fellowship" in our Bible is taken from the New Testament word *koinonia*. Throughout the New Testament, *koinonia* is translated as meaning fellowship, sharing, contribution, association and participation. This kind of relating is a significant concept of the New Testament and expresses shared participation in Christ and the bond that Christ creates between believers. *Koinonia* depicts a harmony between believers that emanates from communion with Christ and the Holy Spirit. In Acts 2:42 we read:

And they continued steadfastly in the apostle's doctrine and fellowship, in the breaking of bread, and in prayers.

As we see in this Acts 2 description of the first church, the believers held *koinonia* in high value. (See also Rom. 15:26; 1 Cor. 1:9; 10:11; 2 Cor. 6:14; 8:4; 9:13; Eph. 2:9; 3:9.)

Most of us contact between 500 and 2,500 acquaintances each year. These acquaintances are people that we don't know in an intimate way; we merely touch their lives in some way. We might even know their names, but we do not spend any intimate time with them. When you go to church and sit beside, take communion with and pray with another believer, you encounter an acquaintance with whom you are enjoying *koinonia*.

KINGDOM PARTNERSHIPS

Kingdom partnerships are relationships that are established by working together in the Kingdom of God. You might not choose a Kingdom partner for a personal friend, or even have parties and picnics with this person; however, you have a partnership with him or her based on the work that you do together for God. Paul had many fellow partners in extending the kingdom of God. For example:

Luke 5:10: James and John, the sons of Zebedee, who were partners with Simon.

Romans: 16:3: Greet Priscilla and Aquilla, my fellow workers in Christ Jesus.

As we get involved in the work of ministering, God will partner us with people who have the gifts, tools and common commitment needed for extending His Kingdom. Most people have from 20 to 100 core friends/partnerships that are regulars whom they know by name. Kingdom partners are people who touch our lives through our jobs, schools, family ties, immediate family connections and friendships in church.

In the New Testament, Kingdom partners are described in terms such as "fellow workers," "fellow laborers," "kinsman," "worker," "companion," "helper" "beloved," "servant," "servant of the church," "helper of many," "my fellow worker in Christ," "my fellow laborer in Christ." All of these terms describe a partnership that has been established because of a ministry that holds a common commitment.

Examples of Kingdom partners include Paul and Barnabas, Paul and Silas, Paul and Aquilla and Priscilla, Paul and Timothy, Paul and Philemon, Jonathan and David. All of these people came together because of the higher purposes they were trying to establish in fulfilling God's will.

In 2 Corinthians 8:23 we read the following about Paul's relationship with Titus:

> If anyone inquires about Titus, he is my partner and fellow worker concerning you. Or if our brethren are inquired about, they are messengers of the churches, the glory of Christ.

(See also Hebrews 10:33; 1 Peter 5:1; 1:4.)

COVENANT RELATIONSHIPS

Covenant relationships form when God joins people together with a commitment that grows into deep, lasting, godly friendships–the kind of friendships that survive in spite of trials, hurts and misunderstandings.

Most people have only one to seven intimate friends or covenant relationships–people they can speak to about anything, at any time, on a level that is not available to the other categories of people. They are friends to die for.

BONDING VERSUS BONDAGE

Friendships are established as we begin to bond with people. And bonding means that we let our emotions and our affections connect with another person. Of course whenever we make ourselves vulnerable to another human being, we risk having our feelings hurt. But when our feelings are hurt, and we do not resolve our conflicts, bonding turns into the bondage of unforgiveness. The result of unforgiveness is lack of intimacy and isolation, which is not the will of God. The Holy Spirit desires to speak with all of us, even at this moment, regarding our relationships. He wants us to be able to bond deeply with people and to know how to deal with those hurts that can come to inhibit us from forming deep relationships.

Friendship is joining together on some level of commitment; it is being mutual in our sharing. The more intimate our relationship, the more we need to share our love and also receive that same degree of love from our friend.

An intimate friend is one that you will stand with and stand beside through thick and thin, knowing that he or she will do the same for you. Someone once said that "a true friend is one who walks in when the others walk out." At our lowest points in life, intimate friends enter into our pain with us. Intimacy may start with a natural affinity for a person, but at some point, a decision is made to bond and go deep. Intimate relationships are a far cry from the American way of making friends for the road, transitory friendships—which come to an end naturally. The road runs out. Life changes. The friends move on. It's not that the friendship failed; it simply transitioned out of your life.

> Someone once said that "a true friend is one who walks in when the others walk out."

As believers, we need to move higher. We can't just have friends of the road so that every time we encounter a bump along the way, we go on to a new relationship. We need friends of the heart who remain with us, even when distance is between us. (See also 1 Thess. 3:12; 1 Cor. 16:14; 2 Pet. 1:7; Gal. 5:22.)

Jesus places friendship and relationships, reconciliation and forgiveness higher than the functioning of our gifts and successes—He puts it higher than worship itself. He said that we are to leave the altar to first pursue Kingdom alignment in our relationships. Jesus knows that every part of our lives will only be as effective as the health of our relationships.

RECONCILIATION

Even the closest relationships sometimes need reconciliation. Reconciliation is altering or removing any problem that hinders the relationship. It is bringing together those who are at variance or at enmity—bringing a healthy change in a relationship that has been damaged. Scripturally, both the offending and the offended parties should seek out reconciliation by exchanging words of forgiveness, dismissing their differences and setting each other free to worship the Lord.

An article in *Psychology Today* magazine entitled "Factors That Lead To a Friendship Ending or Cooling Off" lists 12 common reasons why they do:

- One of us moved.
- I felt that my friend betrayed me.
- We discovered that we had very different views on important issues.
- One of us got married.
- My friend became involved with or married someone I didn't like.
- A friend borrowed money from me.
- I borrowed money from a friend.
- We took a vacation together.
- One of us had a child.
- One of us became markedly more successful at work.
- I got divorced.
- One of us became much richer. [5]

IF YOUR BROTHER HAS SOMETHING AGAINST YOU

We can all relate to one or more of those reasons for having damaged friendships that are in need of reconciliation—most of us could even add to the list. The Bible says that when you know that your brother has something against you, you are to immediately be the first one to make a move toward healing the relationship—whether in your perspective he or she started the problem, or you did. In either case, the initiative is always with you.

When your memory and your conscience hold something against you, you have a Kingdom obligation to judge yourself. However, if a brother or sister is wrongfully offended—offended without cause—

charging you when he or she has no right to do so, then the guilt is on that person and not on you. Nevertheless, to help that individual remove the guilt, you should still attempt to bring reconciliation.

I have worked through the pain of being justly or unjustly hurt, and I can tell you from experience that bearing the brunt of the hurt for the sake of the Kingdom was worth the outcome. Here is one recent example.

We went through a time when some of our seasoned staff pastors made a decision to plant churches in our own metro area. Words cannot communicate what a great challenge this was for me. Until then, we had only planted outside our immediate geographical area and never planted with our own pastors here in Portland. I felt deeply wounded and wondered how this would affect the people in our church as well as all the people who would be leaving. The responses included everything from offense to acceptance. I wanted to cooperate with these men, but it was very difficult.

My heart ached over the fact that they would all plant so nearby, but I also knew that they believed they had heard a call of God to do so. As I sought the Lord, I realized that having a clean, sweet spirit and walking in total forgiveness was far more important to God than having a brother explain himself to me or see the situation from my viewpoint. I knew that if I wanted to maintain Kingdom alignment, I would have to value unity more than my right to being right. I made the choice to let go of my perspectives and decided that the circumstance should be between God and my brothers rather than between God and me. With God's gracious help, I made the decision to serve their vision, not my perspective—and out of that came choice came reconciliation.

In the meantime, I asked the Lord to search my heart and to show me where I needed to take responsibility. I called one of my brothers and confessed that I had not been sensitive to what he truly believed he had heard from God. I acknowledged that he had a right to hear from God. I asked for forgiveness for judging him; I also told him that I would support his decision and do what I could to make him great. The result is that God has flooded my heart with a Kingdom love and desire to bless this fellow pastor and his congregation as well as the other pastors and their congregations. By putting Kingdom values above my own, my values changed—and so will yours.

Reconciliation Precedes Worship
and Ministry

Jesus says reconciliation precedes worship and ministry, but few believers live as though this were true. If we actually practiced this Kingdom principle, can you imagine how it would change the way ministry is done every day? We would definitely have far greater access to the Lord's heart, because according to Matthew 5:23-25, strained relationships can cause our worship to be hindered and even rejected. The reason: The Kingdom is about heart issues. The gift derives its value from the heart of the giver. You can't worship with a pure heart if you have a soiled conscience.

Jesus simply says, "first." In other words, make right relationships a priority. When you've caused a problem, ask to be forgiven. When someone has caused you a problem, forgive. Of course, we cannot control another person's choices. In the best case scenario, your brother or sister should be glad to have you come. He or she should be satisfied with your honest heartfelt confession, demand no more and cheerfully forgive. But if he or she is unreasonable and refuses to forgive you for your part, you still must take responsibility for keeping your own heart free of unforgiveness. The guilt will now rest upon the other party, and the other party only. With the wrong removed from you, you can return to the altar and proceed with offering your gift there.

Will you please take a moment to read Matthew 18:21-35. In this passage Jesus gives a parable about forgiveness. The imagery is borrowed from the old legal method of dealing with debtors who could be put into prison until they paid every cent of their debts. This parable carried the principle of Matthew 5:23-25 to its conclusion.

The Parable of Forgiveness

There are three protagonists in this parable. The first is the debtor, the man who has wronged his brother. He owes a debt of confession and has asked for forgiveness. The second is the creditor, the brother wronged. He too owes a debt–forgiveness. If his brother withholds forgiveness, he remains in debt to the other brother. The final protagonist is the judge. God is the heavenly judge. Both the debtor and creditor will eventually stand before the eternal judge. All things not dealt with biblically through confession, repentance and forgiveness will finally reach His court. Either creditor or debtor will turn the other person over to the judge and leave the other's case to Him.

The punishment for the debtors is prison, a place of torment, a place where people are being limited, held and kept by someone else. The key to reconciliation is humility (see Gal. 6:1)–fully understanding all the ways we can and do fall short of God's glory–something we don't communicate well! Only when we have examined ourselves, can we humbly confront another human being in a manner that will bring about Kingdom alignment. Personal confrontation must precede all other confrontation. To confront means to face someone boldly and openly, eyeball to eyeball, bringing to light that which has caused the offense.

Whether we are the debtor or the creditor, we need to be careful how we handle the problems. Whether we have been wronged or wronged someone else, we still need to go through humble self-examination, confrontation, forgiveness and reconciliation so that we can build our lives upon healthy relationships.
Let's consider Galatians 2:11 and 14:

> Now when Peter had come to Antioch, I withstood him to his face, because he was to be blamed...but when I saw that they were not straightforward about the truth of the gospel, I said to Peter before them all, "If you, being a Jew, live in the manner of Gentiles and not as the Jews, why do you compel Gentiles to live as Jews?

In this passage, we have a first class confrontation between Paul and Peter. Peter was actually guilty and trying to step aside and ignore the situation, but Paul took the issue to a head-on, eyeball-to-eyeball confrontation. Not very face-saving for Peter, but a larger issue was at stake: the very core of the gospel. In this case, there had to be an open and bold refutation.

There is a time to confront in gentleness as we see in Galatians 6:1; there is also a time to confront in Kingdom boldness as we see in

Galatians 2:11,14. The position we take should always be in obedience to God so that He is glorified.

THE FOUNDATION FOR RESTORING RELATIONSHIPS

Forgiveness is not only the foundation for restoring damaged relationships, but it is also the foundation for Kingdom alignment. By forgiveness, I mean giving up resentment, or the desire to punish others. In other words to stop being angry with others, to pardon them, to give up all desire to exact penalties for offenses. Forgiveness means to cancel or remit the debt, fine or penalty.

In Hebrew the word "forgiveness" means to cover over, to lift up or off. It is to send away as the scapegoat was sent into the wilderness with the sins of the people in order to make atonement and pardon for them (see Lev. 16:10). The Greek carries the same idea for forgiveness: to send forth something that is near, to remit, to pardon or to set at liberty or deliverance. Another definition of "forgiveness" incorporates healing others by using their offenses as a means of expressing Christ's love to them.

SIGNS OF UNFORGIVENESS

If unforgiveness is present in a relationship, there will be signs that we can read and hopefully respond to properly. One sign is that the relationship may have waste places (see Isa. 58:12; Lam. 1:10). A waste place means an area where something has dried up or been torn down or pulled down or has become desolate.

There could also be breaches in the relationship (see Isa. 58: 12). A breach is a crack or a gap on a wall that needs repairing, a wound, or an injury, a ruin, a destruction upon something or someone. When there is a breach, it's hard to communicate and hard to respond. It's hard to build any kind of relationship.

A relationship may have divisions (see 1 Cor. 1:10,11). A division is simply a rent or a torn place in the garment where a rip has taken place.

A relationship may have an offense (see Prov. 18:19; Matt. 5:29,30; Rom. 6:10-17). An offense is a stumbling block that has been put in the way so that someone will trip or fall, causing that person to distrust and desert one whom he or she should trust. When offenses are not removed through reconciliation, the relationship will most certainly be damaged and ultimately be ruined.

There may also be some trespasses that occur in the relationship (see Matt. 18:13-15). To trespass simply means to step over another person's stated limits, or boundaries. When a person does not know the other person's boundaries or continually refuses to respect them, deep offenses build, which often lead to bitterness.

Bitterness (see Heb. 12:13-15) is intense animosity that is marked by cynicism and complaints. Out of bitterness comes all kinds of vile emotions.

WHAT FORGIVENESS IS NOT

Forgiveness is not tolerance of evil. It is not looking the other way when sin is done, or making light of wrongs. On the contrary, true forgiveness means there will be a genuine measure of tolerance toward another's weaknesses and foibles, but sin will and must be confronted.

> *"Forgiveness is not just forgetting and pretending that the hurt did not happen. . . It is not making excuses for another person's behavior. It is bringing the hurt into the light so that it can be healed."*

Forgiveness is not just forgetting and pretending that the hurt did not happen. It is not making excuses for another person's behavior. It is bringing the hurt into the light so that it can be healed.

THE COST OF FORGIVENESS

Forgiveness is costly. It can be excruciatingly painful to our emotions and even to our pride. Forgiveness requires love in action, which is the currency of heaven. Forgiveness offers healing medicine to the spirit of both the offended and the offender. Forgiveness is truly the outworking of Christianity in that we bear our cross daily as we die to self-exoneration and do what is right for the sake of the Kingdom.

Building right relationships means building bridges of forgiveness. On one side of the bridge you may have waste places, breaches, divisions, offenses, trespasses and bitterness. You must begin to build a bridge to restore that relationship so that you may be perfectly joined together again. Your bridge-building task will consist of repairing, reconciling, restoring, peacemaking, humbling yourself and taking the first step. We are called to be repairers of the breach, according to Isaiah 58:12; 61:4; 2 Chronicles 24:27; 2 Kings 12:5-12; 22:5. We are to build and make new again; we are to heal and affirm those that we love and should be relating to. Our call is to repair, not to damage; our call is to restore, not to ignore.

We must take on the spirit of Nehemiah who restored the ruins of the walls of Jerusalem. He was moved by what he saw. With weeping and with prayer, he put his faith into action and rebuilt and restored the broken down walls. Nehemiah had a burden to restore the waste places; he became a repairer of the breach. He had to seek out and face the problem before he could restore it. He then revived the stones that were considered unusable, the stones that had been thrown out, and he turned them into usable stones, repairing them and making them rebuildable. We are Nehemiahs in the Body of Christ. We need to be repairers of the breach, restorers of the path and rebuilders of the wall (see Neh. 1:1-3; 2:3-7; 2:5; 2:11-18; Hos. 6:2).

If each and every one of us would chose to become a reconciler in the Body of Christ, we might not always have perfect relationships, but they would be a lot healthier. They would be under repair and under the spirit of restoration instead of under attack and under the spirit of destruction. We are called to be reconcilers of the Body of Christ (see 2 Cor. 5:18,19; Col. 3:13; Eph. 4:31,32). We are called to bring the parties together and mediate if necessary, even though the role of mediator is seldom appreciated. Unity is our best weapon against Satan.

The Bible says that God has given us the ministry of reconciliation and He has given us the word of reconciliation. Will you right now set this book down and begin to pray about those that have damaged you or those you may have wounded. Remember, dear Christian, you have a responsibility. Your responsibility is to take the word of reconciliation with the ministry of reconciliation in the spirit of Christ and thus rebuild those damaged relationships. You are called to be a peacemaker in the Body of Christ (see Matt. 5:9; Rom. 12:18; 1 Thess. 5:13; Col. 3:15).

When it's time to forgive the party that has offended you or that you may have offended, forgive immediately. Forgive when the hurt is first felt, do not delay. Forgive every day during your prayer devotions. Forgive before you are asked to forgive. Forgive with a forgiving spirit and a forgetting spirit. Do not hold on to things, even after you have offered forgiveness. When the cost is staggering, forgive lovingly and forgive finally. Forgive forgetfully and forgive through biblical confession.

Forgiveness can restore the present, heal the future and release the past. Forgiveness can bring healing and reconciliation to all who are involved. Forgiveness can bring release to ministries and deliverance to twisted personalities so that they can become whole again.

Imagine living a life free of offenses. As much as it's up to you, you can. First, be reconciled to your brother. Let forgiveness be first in time, first in value, first on a daily basis. Before anything can be accomplished, before your gift can fully be used in the body of Christ, you must forgive.

Your life can really count in this world today, but you first must learn to live in harmony with others—with your spouse, with your children, with your friends, with your mothers and fathers, with your coworkers, with your neighbors, with fellow Christians, with leaders that God has placed in your life to protect you.

First be reconciled to your brother. If you have been murmuring, complaining, passing on evil and false reports—if you have been making damaging remarks because of unresolved offenses, make a commitment right now that you will no longer live this way. Commit instead to becoming a repairer of the breach, a restorer of paths to walk in, a peacemaker in the Body of Christ. God will honor this commitment, because it is a commitment to Kingdom alignment.

May God richly impart to you His grace and His power to fulfill this law for living, this Kingdom priority. First be reconciled to your brother—then let's offer our gifts together. See you at the altar!

NOTES

1   Story from http://www.fordham.edu/halsall/source/salimbene1.html. The website is maintained by Paul Halsall (ORB sources editor); last modified: January 8, 2000. The Internet Medieval Sourcebook is located at Fordham University Center for Medieval Studies.

2   Michelle Lovric, *Weird Wills & Eccentric Last Wishes* (New York: Barnes and Noble, 2000), p.13.

3   Robert Neely Bellah, William M. Sullivan, Steven M. Tipyon, *Habits of the Heart* (University of California Press, 1985).

4   James Krabill, *Keep the Faith, Share the Peace Newsletter,* (Mennonite Church Peace and Justice Committee, June, 1999) Vol. 5, No. 3, Website: http://www.journeyatowardforgiveness.com/others/James.asp

5   *Psychology Today,* "Factors That Lead To a Friendship Ending or Cooling Off" (Psychology Today, 49 East 21st Street 11th Floor, New York, NY 10010). Unable to locate the author's name or date of the issue.

First Bind the Strong Man
Aligning Your Authority

"Or how can one enter a strong man's house and plunder his goods,
unless he first binds the strong man? And then he will plunder his house."
—Matthew 12:29

Shortly after parking in front of the office, a well-dress businessman
backed into Mr. Bailey's car, causing no more than a slight scratch on
his fender. Mr. Bailey told the man to forget the incident, but the business man insisted on making compensation. He asked for Bailey's
address and promised to send him two tickets to the play. Two weeks
later, the tickets arrived, designating specific seating for a specific date.
Along with the tickets came a box of candy and a gift certificate for
dinner at a plush restaurant near the Performing Arts Center. An entire
night's entertainment was being provided in exchange for a mere scuff
on Mr. Bailey's car. He and his wife were thrilled!

The night was glorious—all it had promised to be—that is, until Mr.
Bailey and his wife returned home. As they pulled into the driveway,
something felt eerie. Then, when they opened the door to the house,
both husband and wife began to sob. They had been duped—unsuspect-
ing victims of a slick thief who had planned their evening so that he
might empty their home of all of its goods and drive away in a fully
packed moving van. This poor couple had been completely taken advantage of because they did not understand the schemes of their enemy.

We can all relate to the Bailey's gutwrenching feelings, because each and every one of us has been robbed in some way by Satan, the strong man who has come "to steal, to kill and to destroy" (John 10:10). In this chapter we will delve into Matthew 12:29 where Jesus gives us our fourth first thing: "First bind the strong man," and then recover stolen goods. According to 2 Corinthians 2:11, we are to be alert "lest Satan should take advantage of us; for we are not ignorant of his devices"—that is, his plots or his specific strategies to ruin our spiritual lives and sabotage our destinies.

Jesus says that we are to "first bind the strong man that we might recover all the goods he has stolen." What has the enemy stolen from you today? Yesterday? Last week? Last month? Last year? In your lifetime? What is due you that you must recover by faith through prayer and the authority of God's Word?

What in your life has your slick enemy, Satan, come "to steal, to kill and to destroy"?

* He comes "to steal": You used to have it, but now it is gone now. He has taken it from you. It no longer exists in your life.

* He comes "to kill": It was alive and flourishing and bearing fruit, but now it is dead.

* He comes "to destroy": There was something in your life that could have been very powerful, but the enemy stopped it, destroyed it, hindered it, crippled it.

It could be any number of things—only you know where you feel ripped off by the strong man. And because God is the Restorer of All Things, I am writing this chapter to assure you that whatever you have lost, part of your Kingdom inheritance is to rightly reclaim it in Christ.

Second Timothy 2:26 says, "That they may come to their senses and escape the snare of the devil, having been taken captive by him to do his will." Where has the devil ensnared you so that you have cooperated with him to do his will? Like the Baileys who played right into the hands of the thief, we often fall for Satan's lies by cooperating with him so that he can steal from us. Therefore, we need help in recovering whatever he has deceptively taken from us.

RECOVER ALL

First Samuel 30:18,19 refers to King David's recovery of all the stolen goods taken from him and his men:

> So David recovered all that the Amalekites had carried away, and David rescued his two wives. And nothing of theirs was lacking, either small or great, sons or daughters, spoil or anything which they had taken from them; David recovered all.

This Scripture along with Matthew 12:29 will become the pilot Scripture for this chapter. We need to believe that, like David, we can recover all and nothing will be lacking, either small or great. Let's pray that the Holy Spirit would begin to stir our hearts with faith to recall even the small and seemingly insignificant things that have been robbed from us—things that according to God's Word are important because without them we cannot completely fulfill the destiny God has for us.

Whether the things the enemy has taken from you are small or great, the promise of the Holy Spirit is to recover ALL.

DELIVERANCE FROM LEGALISM

Jesus teaches us that in order to recover all, we first must bind the strong man before we can plunder his goods:

> "Or how can one enter a strong man's house and plunder his goods, unless he first binds the strong man? And then he will plunder his house" (Matt. 12:29).

Before we discuss specifically Matthew 12:29, let us understand the context in which this Scripture is found. In Matthew 11:28-30, Jesus has made a promise for all who would come to Him, that is to all who would accept Him by faith. He promised rest, including deliverance from the burden of legalism. In the first section of the present chapter (see Matt. 12: 1-14), Jesus explained how belief in Him and His doctrine will deliver people from the yoke of man-made religious traditions. Through His conflict with His opponents, Jesus not only maintained the integrity of His mission but also exposed the inadequacy of their position in relation to the purposes of God.

One cause of the clashes between Jesus and the Pharisees was their legalism. For the Pharisees, keeping the law was an end unto itself; value was sought in the legalistic act rather than in a sense of fidelity to God. But Jesus reminded them of the meaning of the prophetic word which they failed to understand:

> "But you would not have condemned those who aren't guilty if you knew the meaning of this Scripture: 'I want you to be merciful; I don't want your sacrifices'" (Matt. 12:7).

On a certain Sabbath, Jesus' disciples walked through fields of grain, picking a few heads and eating them after rubbing out the kernels with their hands. The Pharisees blamed Jesus for the fact that His disciples had violated the Sabbath rules. But He demolished their criticism and declared Himself to be Lord of the Sabbath. On the Sabbath, He even healed a man with a shriveled hand. This act of restoration occurred in the synagogue, which horrified the Pharisees. Jesus, however, responded with a parable showing that if it was proper to rescue a sheep that had fallen into a pit on the Sabbath, how much more should kindness be shown to a man in need of help on the Sabbath. Christ's rule was: It is right to do good on the Sabbath. The Pharisees reacted by taking counsel against Jesus as to how they might destroy Him.

The law of the Pharisees forbade work on the Sabbath; thus, Jesus' act of healing violated their laws. They had many laws such as forbidding a man to spit on the ground on the Sabbath lest he rub it with his sandal and roll up a ball of dirt, which would be plowing. Another rule forbade a woman to look into the mirror on the Sabbath lest she see a hair in her face and be tempted to fix it.

JESUS AND THE AFFLICTED

In Matthew 12:22-37, we read the account of another person brought to Jesus in dire need. This sorely afflicted man was demon possessed and could neither see nor speak. The Lord performed an astounding triple miracle for him so that the people wondered whether Jesus was the son of David, the Messiah. The enraged Pharisees began accusing Jesus of casting out demons by the power of Beelzebub, that is Satan, the prince of the demons. But Jesus showed that their charge was absurd, inconsistent and untruthful, exposing the wickedness of those who made it.

During the temptation in the wilderness and throughout His ministry, Jesus was in conflict with satanic influences. This conflict was evidenced in His confrontations with demon-possessed individuals; it was also apparent when Jesus entered the wilderness and overcame Satan's temptations. Jesus in effect entered the strong man's house to plunder it of its power.

Jesus said, "But if I cast out demons by the Spirit of God, surely the kingdom of God has come upon you" (Matt. 12:28). Whenever the acts of God are occurring through the power of the Holy Spirit to take back what Satan has twisted or destroyed, the kingdom of God is plundering the strong man's house. But notice that the focus is not on the miracle, it is on the kingdom of God. The emphasis is

> "Whenever the acts of God are occurring through the power of the Holy Spirit to take back what Satan has twisted or destroyed, the kingdom of God is plundering the strong man's house."

on recognizing who Jesus is. When we recognize who really has the power, we are able to enter the battle and take back the power for the Kingdom.

Matthew's account of the man who, because of demonic possession, was blind and mute offers a vivid illustration of Satan's work, which is to limit, bind and blind us. This story simply tells us that Jesus healed him but gives little attention to the actual miracle. Instead, it focuses on the comments of the people as to the possibility that Jesus might actually be the son of David, the Messiah. Faith begins to dawn.

Even though Jesus did not fit their picture of the coming Messiah, His deeds were of such a powerful nature that the people had stirrings of a faith awakening.

The Pharisees, on the other hand, were prejudiced and offered an answer that placed Jesus in league with the prince of devils. The word "Beelzebub" is derived from 2 Kings 1:2 in which Beelzebul (ending in "l") refers to god of Ekron. In 2 Kings 2, the word meant "exalted lord," but in the course of time, the Jews in a little word-play, changed the last letter to "b," making the term "Beelzebub," lord of dung or lord of the flies. By understanding the terms the Pharisees used, we can see their contempt. They used this contemptuous insult in saying that Jesus cast out demons by the power of Beelzebub, prince of demons.

Jesus responded with a series of logical arguments. First, if He were casting out demons with the help of the ruler of demons, then the demonic kingdom was self-destructing. Second, the Jews themselves practiced exorcism, so they must be succeeding by demonic power— hence, they were condemning themselves. And third, if He were casting out demons, which they had admitted by their statements, then it must be evidenced that He had entered the strong man's house and had defeated the strong man.

"Jesus' defeat of Satan in the wilderness, through His authority as God's Son, enabled Him to cast out demons with the Word. His authority and methods stood in contrast to the extensive and strange exercises of the Jewish exorcists." [1]

JESUS IS THE DELIVERER

Jesus is the Deliverer. He comes to bring freedom from internal and external bondages—from past, present and future bondages. He brings freedom to people, especially delivering them from obvious emotional and physical snares of the enemy.

When Jesus says, "How can one enter a strong man's house and plunder his goods, unless he first binds the strong man? And then he will plunder his house" (Matt. 12:9), He is underscoring His argument of verse 28 with a parable. He compares Satan to the master of the house and the demon-possessed to household articles. Jesus bases His argument upon the common beliefs that Satan is a powerful spirit and that the spirits can only be cast out by stronger spirits. Jesus overcomes and defeats Satan through the power of the kingdom of God and by the power of the Holy Spirit.

BINDING

The Greek word *deo* means to bind, to tie, to forbid. In pagan minds, "bind" was used to describe the power exercised over someone by either a sorcerer, a god or a spirit. Release from that spirit was called "loosing," setting that person free and removing the power of that binding over his or her life. In Matthew 18:18 Jesus said, "Assuredly, I say unto you, whatever you bind (*deo*) on earth will be bound in heaven, and whatever you loose on earth will be loosed in heaven."

THE STRONG MAN

The Greek word for "strong" used in Matthew 12:29 is *ischuros*, meaning someone who is strong, powerful, mighty, able and forcible. A key aspect of *ischuros* is its intensity. This word is pictured as a violent wind or an army's force. The Old Testament cognate word is used for a severe famine or a woman bitterly weeping or an army being totally defeated. Clearly, this word describes the power of the enemy upon a person's life, which comes in like a mighty force as a violent wind to attack and to ruin it.

In 1 Peter 5:8,9 we are exhorted to "be sober, be vigilant; because your adversary the devil walks about like a roaring lion, seeking whom he may devour. Resist him, steadfast in the faith, knowing that the same sufferings are experienced by your brotherhood in the world." To resist means to stand against—that is, to firmly plant your feet in opposition. Ephesians 4:27 says, "Give no place to the devil." The enemy comes to entrap us, to wrap his cords around our feet and around our souls (see Prov. 5:22; John 8:36; 2 Tim. 2:25,26).

THE STRONG MAN, THE PRINCE OF THIS WORLD

Jesus describes the strong man as the prince of this world. The word "prince" is the word *archon*, denoting the highest official of the city or region in the Greco-Roman world. Jesus refers to the *archon* in several verses:

> John 12:31: "Now is the judgment of this world; now the ruler (the *archon*) of this world will be cast out."

> John 14:30: "I will no longer talk much with you, for the ruler (the *archon*) of this world is coming and has nothing in me."

> John 16:11: "And of judgment because the ruler (the *archon*) of this world is judged.

First John 5:19 is an amazing verse—one that needs to be carefully considered as the believer seeks understanding:

> We are of God, and the whole world lies under the sway of the wicked one.

The apostle simply says that the whole world is under his influence. The possibility of bringing bondage upon the world because of his influence and sway is a reality. The enemy comes to blind all people's minds so they cannot see how to get free from his bondage. Read the following verses carefully:

> 2 Corinthians 4:4: Whose minds the god of this age has blinded, who do not believe, lest the light of the gospel of the glory of Christ, who is the image of God, should shine on them.

> Ephesians 2:2: In which you once walked according to the course of this world, according to the prince of the power of the air, the spirit who now works in the sons of disobedience.

We were once under the power and spirit of deception, which the devil had over our lives as unbelievers. But as we came under the blood of Christ, these things were broken from our lives positionally so that we now can begin to move from our position into a practice of living out our deliverance. Jesus states that a person cannot make the significant headway necessary in taking back the property of this kingdom unless he or she first ties up the strong man.

BINDING THE STRONG MAN

Jesus' whole ministry was about overpowering the fully armed strong man who guarded his property, namely God's people—and ultimately the entire earth (see Mark 3:27; Luke 11:21,22). Note: Though the earth is the Lord's positionally (see Ps. 24:1), the activity upon the earth is not always of the Lord. Earth, therefore, is the battleground, and we are the goods.

Jesus was successful in breaking into the strong man's house—people's lives—and casting out demons, delivering people from bondage. His whole ministry was about tying up the strong man. Acts 10:38 says that "God anointed Jesus of Nazareth with the Holy Spirit and with power, who went about doing good and healing all who were oppressed by the devil, for God was with him."

SICKNESS, SATAN'S SCHEME

In Luke 13:11 we read about "a woman who had a spirit of infirmity eighteen years, and was bent over and could in no way raise herself up." This woman was healed and delivered by Jesus so that she was able to stand up straight and walk normally. What happened to this infirmed woman can happen to all of us who were once under the power of the enemy and have come fully under the power of Christ. We can receive total and complete healing.

Luke 13:16 refers to this woman as "a daughter of Abraham whom Satan has bound." Imagine being bound for 18 years, and then being loosed from that bondage—on the Sabbath to boot! Jesus treated sickness and deformity and diseases of all sorts as being part of Satan's scheme to tie up God's people. He brought salvation and deliverance, not just spiritual regeneration. Jesus brought deliverance from the evil grasp of sickness and from the dominion of Satan (see Mark 3:10; 9:25).

Jesus did not try to discern some secret sovereign divine blueprint behind all diseases. He simply treated them as being inflicted by Satan. Let me point out that because He is sovereign, Jesus can use even the most dreadful events inflicted on our lives by Satan, including sickness, to redeem something we have lost.

I can't help but think of Joni Erickson Tada, who in 1967 had a diving accident that left her a quadriplegic. From that time on she has been confined to a wheelchair, unable to use her hands. Nonetheless, she is a wife, an incredible artist—painting with a brush between her teeth—an author of 27 books, a columnist for *Moody Monthly* magazine, an internationally known singer, radio-show host, an international film star of the World Wide Pictures' movie "JONI," and founder of Joni and Friends, an international ministry to the disabled. Joni has affected more people in her wheelchair than most of us will with full use of all of our limbs. Did the strong man plunder Joni's life? Yes. But he has been bound, and Jesus has recovered the goods.

When the enemy steals from you, you may not always recover what you lost in the same form that you lost it, but you will recover it with a greater sense of glory than before.

I have seen people who have been through deliverance from tormenting demons, and they are not the same. When the glory of the Lord shines upon them, they take on the appearance of an overcomer. In Mark 5:2-13 we see the overcoming power of Jesus Christ:

And when He had come out of the boat, immediately there met Him out of the tombs a man with an unclean spirit, who had his dwelling among the tombs; and no one could bind him, not even with chains, because he had often been bound with shackles and chains. And the chains had been pulled apart by him, and the shackles broken in pieces; neither could anyone tame him. And always, night and day, he was in the mountains and in the tombs, crying out and cutting himself with stones. When he saw Jesus from afar, he ran and worshiped Him. And he cried out with a loud voice and said, "What have I to do with You, Jesus, Son of the Most High God? I implore You by God that You do not torment me." For He said to him, "Come out of the man, unclean spirit!" Then He asked him, "What is your name?" And he answered, saying, "My name is Legion; for we are many." Also he begged Him earnestly that He would not send them out of the country. Now a large herd of swine was feeding there near the mountains. So all the demons begged Him, saying, "Send us to the swine, that we may enter them." And at once Jesus gave them permission. Then the unclean spirits went out and entered the swine (there were about two thousand); and the herd ran violently down the steep place into the sea, and drowned in the sea.

This passage from Mark clearly shows the power of the Lord Jesus in delivering and casting out many demons. Whenever Christ comes in contact with the enemy's power, the result is that Christ's power overcomes (see Matt. 9:32,33; Luke 7:21).

POWER TO BIND THE STRONG MAN

Jesus has given the believer power and authority to tie up the strong man just as He Himself has tied up the strong man:

Luke 10:19: "Behold, I give you the authority to trample on serpents and scorpions (satanic spirits), and over all the power of the enemy, and nothing shall by any means hurt you."

In Matthew 28:18 Jesus says, "All authority has been given to Me in heaven and on earth," and Jesus turns around and gives that authority to us.

The word "power" in the Greek is *dunamos*, used here regarding Satan's power and Satan's might and ability. The word "authority" is *exousia* in Greek, which is the right to act; it is delegated authority. All of God's power and authority is behind the believer when he or she acts on behalf of the Kingdom.

Because Jesus has bound the strong man, the Church is positioned to plunder his house. Matthew 12:29 says that Jesus is building His Church and that it will be triumphant over the kingdom of darkness. The mission of the Church is to rescue unbelievers who are under the dominion of the kingdom of darkness (see Matt. 16:18; Acts 26:17,18).

Jesus Christ has won the complete victory over Satan. He defeated Satan in his life and ministry (see Matt. 4:11). He defeated Satan in His substitutionary death on the Cross (see Col. 2:14,15). He defeated Satan in His resurrection and ascension to the throne of God (see Heb. 4:14).

In the end, only the kingdom of God will remain on the earth, and the Church, empowered by the Holy Spirit, will have been the vehicle used to establish that Kingdom (see Eph. 1:22,23; 3:10,11). As citizens of the kingdom of God, we participate in the victory of Jesus Christ because we are seated with Christ in a position of authority (see Eph. 2:2,6). We have been given authority to cast out evil spirits (see Mark 16:17, Luke 10:19). We have been given authority to defeat all the works of darkness (see Rom. 16:20)—although it might take redemptive suffering, or even a real cross such as that of the Christians in the Sudan, to overcome.

Believers are to be alert (see 1 Pet. 5:8), submitting to God and resisting the devil (see Jas. 4:7). We have been given spiritual weapons (see Eph. 6:12,13) and the ability to tear down strongholds (see 2 Cor. 10:3,4). Casting out evil spirits can be a sign of the coming of the kingdom of God in power (see Luke 11:20).

RECOVER ALL THE ENEMY HAS TAKEN

"Satan uses the power of manipulation and deception to steal from us, but we are to use the power of truth to recover all that the enemy has taken."

The spiritual mandate is to recover all, small and great, by the power of the Holy Spirit. Nothing the enemy has tried to steal from us belongs to him because he is a thief. God has already bought these things and put them in our house, in our spiritual dwellings, by the power of the cross, the blood of Jesus Christ and the Holy Spirit.

Satan uses the power of manipulation and deception to steal from us, but we are to use the power of truth to recover all that the enemy has taken.

One thing the enemy tried to steal from my wife, Sharon, and I is our children. For years, we struggled with the pain of barrenness, submitting to all kinds of embarrassing and annoying medical tests. We also received prophetic words of promise from prophets around the world—still nothing happened. We finally sought to increase our family through adoption, thinking it would be easy—it was not. Many trials ensued before we received the miracle of our two awesome adopted daughters, and many more occurred before our home was filled with the two mercy gifts of our biological son and daughter. Victory is ours! We not only recovered what the enemy stole from us, but we were also multiplied in who we became and what we received in the process.

To recover means that we need to snatch it away from the enemy's hand. We need to defend, deliver, escape without fail. We need to pluck it up, rescue, spoil and take back what the enemy has done. We need to fight for it. We need to walk in a spirit of restoration and bring that spirit to others. To restore means to reestablish to the condition that God has already established in His written Word. It means a condition of health, making good the breaking of the stone by a workman, by his substituting another; to mend something torn, to repair a broken vessel. Restoration is our job as believers.

Both corporate intercession (which is praying in concert with other believers) and repentance (which is taking responsibility for our sins) are very effective in pushing back the authority of the kingdom of darkness. According to Matthew 16:19, the Church has been given the keys of the Kingdom of heaven. Keys imply unlocking. We have the keys to the doors where Satan has hidden the goods. Our Kingdom keys give us authority to bind—in other words to tie, fasten, hinder, put under obligation, constrain, forbid, prohibit, declare to be illicit. We are to loose, that is to unlock, untie, unfasten, unbind, release from bonds, set free, discharge from prison, dissolve, annul, deprive of authority.

It is the Church's rightful role to advance the authority of God's kingdom and subvert the authority of Satan's kingdom. In this process, however, the Kingdom of heaven, the throne of God, continues to be in control. The Church responds to heaven's initiative. In Matthew 18 the words "bind" and "loose" are in the perfect tense, referring to an action that happens in the past but the effects of which continue into the present. The Church's present binding and loosing are the result of the binding and loosing already declared in heaven.

Ultimately the battle is not ours, but the Lord's (see 2 Chron. 20:15). When Jesus leads the Church in the battle, it is always triumphant because the war has already been won. (See Luke 10:18,19; John 12:31; Rom. 16:20; 2 Cor. 10:3,4; 2 Tim. 2:26; 1 John 3:8; Rev. 12:10.) There are, of course, ongoing battles that we are still cleaning up by the power of the Holy Spirit. And though the Holy Spirit would challenge us to recover all things by the power and authority of the Lord Jesus Christ, we live in a fallen world where God's will is not always implemented.

With that said, let's consider 12 things, the Lord would have us recover. Undoubtedly, the recovering process needs to be quickened by the Holy Spirit in each one of our lives; He will pinpoint exactly what things you and I should recover and where the process should begin for us—but the following list of 12 contains some of the most obvious. I encourage every believer to use these 12 recovery items as a prayer list for awhile, praying the corresponding verses along with the other Scriptures that I have mentioned in this chapter.

You have the authority to recover all that the enemy has taken from you. Believe that 1 Samuel 30:18,19 belongs to YOU:

So David recovered all.

Right now, declare, "So David recovered all." Then pray this prayer out loud:

Holy Spirit, I believe that You want me to recover all. Small or great, I believe You will help me to recover these things into my life, into my family and into the world I live in.

Now as you have prayed this prayer, believe that the Holy Spirit will anoint you as you read so that you will advance with Kingdom authority and faith to charge into the house that has already been plundered and simply take back the goods that belong to you.

TWELVE THINGS TO RECOVER

1. Recover the relationships that the enemy has sought to destroy.

Isaiah 58:12: Those from among you shall build the old waste places; you shall raise up the foundations of many generations; and you shall be called the Repairer of the Breach, the Restorer of Streets to Dwell In.

Recover relationships between husband and wife, parents and children, children and children, employer and employee, friend and friend, sons and daughters. Believe that all relationships that belong in your life will be restored to the place that God can use these relationships to build His Kingdom. The enemy comes to steal, to kill and to destroy your relationships but you can take them back.

2. Recover personal promises that God has given you through Scripture.

2 Corinthians 1:20: For all the promises of God in Him are Yes, and in Him Amen, to the glory of God through us.

Hebrews 11:33: Who through faith subdued kingdoms, worked righteousness, obtained promises, stopped the mouths of lions,

The promises you have received are probably in your Bible, circled Scriptures, notes written in the margin, or maybe they came in letters sent by friends or relatives. They are Scriptures associated with a promise—for example, that you should believe for healing, or restoration, or that a prodigal child will return to the house of God. Perhaps you've had a promise concerning your business, your finances, your job or being released into a different level of faith, a different realm of walking in the kingdom of God. Look at the Scriptures the Lord has given you throughout the years. Every believer should have key promises in the Scriptures, and now is the your time to recover them.

The following testimony of intercessor Beverly McIntyre recorded in the book *Intercessors, Discover Your Prayer Power* illustrates how we reclaim our promises regarding our children:

> My daughter was unmercifully chided and teased about her weight as a child and grew up with a lot of shame regarding her body. Later, in her teen years, Satan finally wrenched a deadly grip on her life. Though the pendulum swung back and forth between bulimia and anorexia, it began at age 16 when Crystan started bingeing and purging....
>
> Finally, when Crystan turned 22, I faced one of the darkest days of my life. My husband and I checked our daughter into a secular clinic that secured her behind locked doors. Leaving that hospital, I felt devastated over her pain and my inability to intervene with a solution. For several days I did nothing but sob. I knew at that point that our only hope was Jesus. As I cried out to God, the Lord impressed me to pray Isaiah 54. Throughout three of the four weeks of her hospital stay, I walked the floors for a minimum of eight hours daily, proclaiming Isaiah 54 over her life and declaring that bulimia and anorexia would have to bow to the name of Jesus. One day, a peace eclipsed my pain, and I knew the work had been done in the heavenlies.

The time Crystan spent in the clinic had steeled her feelings of anger toward me and everything I represented. My daughter returned home embittered and hardened to the things of God. For three months I simply rested in the peace God had given me. Suddenly, at about 2 A.M., I was awakened by the sounds of weeping as my daughter discreetly tiptoed into my bedroom. "Mom," she sighed, "come and hear what the Lord just spoke to me." I followed her to the kitchen and listened attentively as she read Isaiah 54 from the *Amplified Bible*. I did not tell her then nor did she have any idea that not only was this the same Scripture I had prayed over her, but it was also the same version I had used. Crystan crawled into my lap, and God healed her that very night. It was a defining moment for both of us.

Today when people tell me they have addicted children at home, I encourage them not to become sedated by victimization but to rise up with mercy and fight. Draw a line in the sand and tell Satan he can't cross over it, because God has given you the authority to fight in His name. Become a prayer weapon for God until that child experientially walks in the victory of Isaiah 54:13: "All your children shall be taught by the LORD, and great shall be the peace of your children" (NKJV). No one will ever love your child as much as you do. You are the one who is called to pay the price in prayer. Find a Scripture and stand upon its truth until the Lord gives you the assurance that the breakthrough has happened. Don't give up. Don't look at what you see. Instead, stand upon the Word and focus upon the Lord's power. Trust God to save your family. [2]

3. Recover prophetic words the enemy has stolen.

Psalm 105:19: Until the time that his word came to pass, the word of the LORD tested him.

Prophetic words can come in many different forms: quickenings, dreams, words given through proven leaders, or counsel. Prophetic words are words that are quickened in our hearts, revealing some aspect of the future that God wants us to lay hold on. Now let me ask you: what prophetic words have quickened in your heart? What prophetic words regarding your future have you given up on? Recover those prophetic words. Get them out if you have them. Then, write them down and read them again. If you can, talk with people who have prayed prophetic prayers over you, and ask them to pray them again. Recover even the strangeness of some of the words concerning your future that now seem far removed, but can be reclaimed with faith.

When Sharon and I were walking through our barren years, we held on to the prophetic words we received. Eventually, we saw God bring them to pass in greater ways than we could have imagined.

4. Recover the spirit of faith that perseveres until it overcomes.

> Romans 1:17: For in it the righteousness of God is revealed from faith to faith; as it is written, "The just shall live by faith."

> Matthew 9:29: Then He touched their eyes, saying, "According to your faith let it be to you."

To recover your faith, you bend your knee in prayer and open your heart to a new stirring of God's greatness. Compile a list of at least 20 faith Scriptures (see Appendix A) and begin to read them out loud. Read through the list often; you might even want to memorize it. Meditate on some of the mighty acts of God, not only in Scripture but also in your own life. Speak faith, telling others of both the providential and supernatural miracles that you've experienced, the big ones and the small ones. Begin to stir a spirit of faith again by believing the biblical promises and prophetic words you've received. Speak faith. Remove unbelief and doubt and any negative words that you've been repeating. Restore faith to your spirit by taking some simple faith steps right now, today.

Then, when you have truly released your faith, God will bring the answer in ways that you never imagined. I am not saying that the answers will always come neatly wrapped in a pretty, cushy package, but they will come wrapped in the grace of God and tied to a Kingdom promise that your reward will be great.

God has a timing for every answered prayer, as long as it is offered in faith. The following story of Xu Yonghai's imprisonment in Mainland China demonstrates God's power to multiply today's seeds of faith for tomorrow's harvest.

Xu Yonghai looked around his 8-by-8-foot cell. A trained medical doctor, Yonghai was accustomed to sanitized conditions, so what he saw was especially disgusting. There was no bathroom—only a pipe in one corner of the cell from which water flowed continuously onto the concrete. Yonghai learned to use the pipe to wash human waste from his cell. He drank and washed himself with water from the pipe. He also ate right there when guards slipped his food under the door.

Not once in two years did Xu leave his tiny, filthy room!

Yonghai, a Christian in Communist China, had worked with Gao Feng to legalize a house church. For this "crime," he was locked up in a Beijing prison for 24 months. Yonghai spent much of his imprisonment in prayer and meditation—and writing. On the walls of his cell, Yonghai scrawled the major points for a book, *God the Creator*. He wrote with soap—his deep-thinking, intellectual mind tying the points of his theses together. When the writing was finished, Yonghai memorized the words. After his release in May 1997, he put his cell-wall composition on paper. The result was a 50,000-word book!

"My cell was the last stop for prisoners sentenced to die," Yonghai said. "At times there were as many as three other prisoners in the tiny, damp room, awaiting their date with the executioner."

What a chance to witness! What an opportunity to introduce these men to God's kingdom! Yonghai took advantage of his situation, sharing the Gospel with his temporary cellmates in their final days on earth. He reports, "These men were very open to the message of Christ."

"My living conditions were deplorable, but after four months, the Lord helped me to adapt. God was with me, even in my darkest times, helping me endure my years in prison. Only God gave me the strength to do it."

As demonstrated by Xu Yonghai, faith may mean enduring hard times, but God will use the test to provide us with a greater testimony! Yonghai's faith in God lit the path for others who were seeking eternal life; it also became the launching pad to his future as a writer. We don't always know where our faith will take us, but we do know the One who will be with us all the way.

5. Recover the miracles of healing and deliverance.

> Jeremiah 30:17: "For I will restore health to you and heal you of your wounds," says the LORD, "Because they called you an outcast saying: 'This is Zion; no one seeks her.'"

> Acts 6:8: Stephen, full of faith and power, did great wonders and signs among the people.

God is seeking to stir up the Body of Christ, beginning with you, to believe for the miracles of healing and deliverance from every kind of bondage. Maybe you've had a theological problem with the reality of miracles and you've refused to consider the potential of God's healing power in your body. Reread the account of Jesus' ministry in Scripture. This time, however, notice how much Jesus was involved in setting people free from every kind of disease and personality disorder. He used healing as one of His main tools for restoring Kingdom alignment to people's lives.

A read through the book of Acts will confirm that the Early Church often moved in the realm of healing and freedom from demonic influences in people's lives. We've been given the same authority with gifts of healing for today; we are also to counsel and to bring deliverance to people's lives. Let us recover the miracles of healing and setting people free from oppressive, twisting and tormenting spirits.

Even if you are discouraged with some lack of healing or some lack of deliverance from something that is affecting your emotional life, do not step backward. Step forward. Let's take some ground from the enemy. Let us recover all, small and great.

6. Recover financial prosperity.

> Psalm 129:8: "The blessing of the LORD be upon you; we bless you in the name of the LORD!"

> Proverbs 10:22: The blessing of the Lord makes one rich, and He adds no sorrow with it.

Malachi 3:10: Bring all the tithes into the storehouse, that there may be food in My house, and try Me now in this, says the Lord of hosts, if I will not open for you the windows of heaven and pour out for you such blessing that there will not be room enough to receive it.

We believe that the blessing of the Lord is upon us and that we can bless as we have been blessed. Financial prosperity is something that many believers lack. It could be that you are presently in a financially bankrupt position, or in a position of financial instability. Perhaps blessing and prosperity are foreign words to you—you scarcely make ends meet. Let me encourage you once again to search the Scriptures. Find out what the Bible says about finances and prosperity, including greed and envy. My perspective is guided a lot by the book of Proverbs. Why not build your own faith for financial blessing and financial stability?

Begin with being faithful in the least, in the giving of your tithes to the house of God, the storehouse. Then begin to stretch out and give offerings. As you sow, so shall you shall reap. As you give, the blessings of the Lord will overtake you.

The enemy comes to rob us of positive attitudes and rob us of God's promises to us. He deceives us from believing the truth that the Word of God is faithful and that God really does want to pour out a blessing upon us that is so great we can't even contain it. I challenge you to rise up and believe God, believe His Word. Will you believe that there's a blessing waiting for you, right above your head, a giant bowl that God just wants to tip and pour all over you? Unleash your faith to recover all, both small and great, that the enemy has taken from you financially.

7. Recover the joy of the Lord.

Nehemiah 8:10: Then he said to them, "Go your way, eat the fat, drink the sweet, and send portions to those for whom nothing is prepared; for this day is holy to our LORD. Do not sorrow, for the joy of the LORD is your strength."

Psalm 30:5: For His anger is but for a moment, His favor is for life; weeping may endure for a night, but joy comes in the morning.

Psalm 51:12: Restore to me the joy of Your salvation, and uphold me by Your generous Spirit.

Scripture promises the joy of the Lord, a joy that will transcend our physical and emotional circumstances. The joy of the Lord is to be our strength. The joy of the Lord is to come upon us with a generous spirit. God will not withhold the joy of the Lord; He pours out grand portions of joy upon us and in us, so that we might become joyful people.

Evangelist Billy Sunday once said, "If you have no joy in your religion, there's a leak in your Christianity somewhere." What has robbed you of your joy? What has caused you to be a bit pessimistic—even a little depressed, mean, rude or irritable? Do you frown more than you smile? Or speak discouraging words more than encouraging words? Has the laughter valve been shut off in your life? Do you enjoy good times with friends or family? If not, will you ask God to help you recover your joy in both small and great things today? Your joy is your strength. Begin to quote Scriptures on joy. Spend some time in prayer asking God to show you about joy. Allow joy to permeate your speech until you become infected with it. By changing your attitude, you can change your life—so let the joy of the Lord be your strength.

8. Recover the wasted years.

Joel 2:25: So I will restore to you the years that the swarming locust has eaten, the crawling locust, the consuming locust, and the chewing locust, my great army which I sent among you.

Psalm 106:43: Many times he delivered them, but they were bent on rebellion and they wasted away in their sin (*NIV*).

Years could have been wasted because of the enemy's treacherous attack upon your life. He comes to sweep clean all those good things represented by the locusts who came upon the land to totally devour every part of it, the swarming locust, the crawling locust, the consuming locust and chewing locust.

Hear the promises of the Lord:

"I would give you back the years the locust has stolen. I will recompense you for the years that the swarmer has eaten. I will pay you back for the profitless years when sin ravaged you as the enemy came in like the locusts. I will now restore those years to your life."

The enemy thrives on taking advantage of our sins and foibles, causing us to lose time in our relationships, in our marriages, with our children, in our jobs and ministries, and with our own spiritual progress. It is so discouraging to wake up and realize that you have wasted 5, 10 or more years by not dealing with your personal flaws such as lack of spiritual discipline, lack of love, bad attitudes and setting a poor example for your family. You feel like the locusts have come in and licked you clean, swarmed your home and your life, crawled all over your belongings and consumed your life. Don't beat yourself up. Instead, know that your wake-up call is a miracle from God to keep you from wasting any more years. As you come to your senses in true repentance, God will restore the wasted years if you cooperate with Him. He can bring fruitfulness out of unfruitful years, and He wants to double your blessings so that the latter years are greater than the former.

9. Recover the cities the enemy has taken.

1 Samuel 7:12-14: Then Samuel took a stone and set it up between Mizpah and Shen, and called its name Ebenezer, saying, "Thus far the LORD has helped us." So the Philistines were subdued, and they did not come anymore into the territory of Israel. And the hand of the LORD was against the Philistines all the days of Samuel. Then the cities which the Philistines had taken from Israel were restored to Israel, from Ekron to Gath; and Israel recovered its territory from the hands of the Philistines. Also there was peace between Israel and the Amorites.

2 Kings 20:6: And I will add to your days fifteen years. I will deliver you and this city from the hand of the king of Assyria; and I will defend this city for My own sake, and for the sake of My servant David.

Let us rise up with the great challenge of recovering the twenty-first-century cities that have been enslaved by the multiple complexities of our enemy's strategies to destroy people. Satan has infiltrated our cities with violence, immorality, sensuality, homosexuality and confusion—all the things that would totally ruin and wreck a city. We must have faith that God wants to restore our cities. I am so convinced of this that I have devoted an entire book to the subject: *Crossing Rivers and Taking Cities.* Another good book on this subject is Ed Silvoso's *That None Should Perish.*

Cities are restored as we prayerwalk our neighborhoods and believe with faith that God can and will move there. I want to encourage you to connect with at least one other believer today, a believer who will prayerwalk with you. Then, begin to pray the following prayer over your city:

Father,

In the Name of Jesus Christ of Nazareth, let Thy Kingdom come, let Thy will be done in [insert your city's name]. We stand against the spirits that are warring against our city and region. We bind the spirits of rebellion, religious deception, blasphemy, immorality and witchcraft over [insert your city's name]. Father God, release Your warring angels and release the Holy Spirit to do warfare against these enemies. Set revival fires to burn hot in Your church in this city. Send revival to this region. Release a spirit of repentance over [insert your city's name]. Fill your church with compassion and mercy. Let the spirit of prayer intercession rest upon all congregations in [insert your city's name]. Let us, by Your grace, make a difference in our generation in this place for we are the planting of the Lord here. In Jesus' mighty name, we pray.

Amen

10. Recover the lambs or sheep stolen from the flock.

> 1 Samuel 17:34-37: But David said to Saul, "Your servant used to keep his father's sheep, and when a lion or a bear came and took a lamb out of the flock, I went out after it and struck it, and delivered the lamb from its mouth; and when it arose against me, I caught it by its beard, and struck and killed it. Your servant has killed both lion and bear; and this uncircumcised Philistine will be like one of them, seeing he has defied the armies of the living God." Moreover David said, "The Lord, who delivered me from the paw of the lion and from the paw of the bear, He will deliver me from the hand of this Philistine." And Saul said to David, "Go, and the Lord be with you!"

> 1 Samuel 30:20: Then David took all the flocks and herds they had driven before those other livestock, and said, "This is David's spoil."

The lambs represent people who are spiritually immature in God's flock. The sheep are those who have grazed among us for many years. Now the enemy has stolen them from the flock. He has swept down onto the plains from the mountains and taken those who were slow and crippled. He has stalked and stolen those with a wandering attitude, wandering from the flock. He has deceived them, driving them off a spiritual cliff somewhere.

But we should rise up with a spirit of faith and restoration for the lambs and the sheep that have been stolen from our local churches. Some of these people move from one church to another, not knowing how to make a commitment, so they never feel familied by the body of Christ. Others, leave a particular church and never end up making an effort to reconnect anywhere else. Instead, they stumble and fall and remove themselves entirely from the flock of God. As someone has glibly stated, "Remember the banana—when it left the bunch, it got skinned." And skinned they are—spiritually skinned.

Can you think of friends, family members or disciples who have been stolen from the flock and spiritually skinned? Maybe you never wrote to them, prayed for them or went after them; you didn't even phone or visit them. The Holy Spirit wants to stir your spirit right now to restore those stolen lambs and sheep; He wants to infuse you with the faith needed to go after them. Will you go for Jesus' sake?

11. Recover the blessing of God on our homes and families.

Deuteronomy 11:18-21: Therefore you shall lay up these words of mine in your heart and in your soul, and bind them as a sign on your hand, and they shall be as frontlets between your eyes. You shall teach them to your children, speaking of them when you sit in your house, when you walk by the way, when you lie down, and when you rise up. And you shall write them on the doorposts of your house and on your gates, that your days and the days of your children may be multiplied in the land of which the LORD swore to your fathers to give them, like the days of the heavens above the earth.

Deuteronomy 28:2-4: And all these blessings shall come upon you and overtake you, because you obey the voice of the LORD your God: Blessed shall you be in the city, and blessed shall you be in the country. Blessed shall be the fruit of your body, the produce of your ground and the increase of your herds, the increase of your cattle and the offspring of your flocks.

Proverbs 3:33: The curse of the LORD is on the house of the wicked, but He blesses the home of the just.

Proverbs 9:9,10: Give instruction to a wise man, and he will be still wiser; teach a just man, and he will increase in learning. The fear of the LORD is the beginning of wisdom, and the knowledge of the Holy One is understanding.

The Lord wants us to experience the recovered blessing of God upon each and every home and each and every family. God has promised that He will allow the richness of His Word and His Spirit to dwell in our homes in such a way that it will encourage our children, producing godly offspring. We know that the enemy comes in to steal, to kill and to destroy, especially the young of the flock–our children, our teenagers and our young adults. Every stage of our children's lives, therefore, needs to be carefully watched and strategically pastored.

We parents must keep both hands on the wheel, continuously scrutinizing each child's life in order to help each one stay on a godly path. You and I must make sure that the enemy does not steal even one lamb from our homes.

Do not allow yourself to release your kids when they are young adults, saying, "Whatever happens happens." It is more important for you as a parent to be involved on a daily basis with prayer and wisdom when your child reaches young adulthood than at any other time in his or her life. Spend time with your child to discuss anything and everything, including jobs, education, dating, moving or any other important decision. My caution is: Parents, do not remove yourself too soon. In counseling, I often find that mothers and fathers have simply backed off too quickly and too much, leaving a vacuum in their children's lives, especially with their older children. (See Appendix B for more information of raising healthy children.)

Perhaps you're thinking, *But the enemy has already stolen from our home*. Recover the stolen goods–the stolen relationship that has been taken from you, whether it is a relationship between you and your child or between you and your spouse. Recover the stolen time that the enemy has robbed from you due to busyness, work or recreation as you neglected to spend quality time building your relationships.

Recover, restore–don't give up on those relationships. The love and the commitment can be rekindled, you just need to blow upon that flame and cause it to burn again. We are here to recover everything that the Lord has spoken to us concerning our families.

11. Recover the blessing of God upon our nation.

Deuteronomy 4:5-7: Surely I have taught you statutes and judgments, just as the LORD my God commanded me, that you should act according to them in the land which you go to possess. Therefore be careful to observe them; for this is your wisdom and your understanding in the sight of the peoples who will hear all these statutes, and say, "Surely this great nation is a wise and understanding people." For what great nation is there that has God so near to it, as the LORD our God is to us, for whatever reason we may call upon Him?

Proverbs 14:34: Righteousness exalts a nation, but sin is a reproach to any people.

There is currently an unprecedented amount of prayer being offered up on behalf of the United States of America, probably more than at any time in the past 200 years. Prayer cards, prayer centers, prayer houses and prayer congregations are emerging on the forefront all across this land as people prayerfully ask God to bless our nation, to remove the wickedness, to uproot the rebellion, to protect us from terrorists, to heal our land and to restore us as a society and as a great nation under God. And God is answering our prayers. President George W. Bush is a praying president who is boldly standing for God before the entire nation.

The Bible says that when the righteous are in authority, the people rejoice (see Prov. 29:2). Therefore, let us intercede for our president and our country. Let our intercession be done with joy and faith. Let it be done with a spirit of hope and perseverance. Let it be done in agreement with the numerous biblical promises that assure us that God wants to bless America.

RECAPPING

As we conclude this chapter, let's pause again to reconsider the points we have covered and pray about them. This book is intended to be more than a classroom textbook, it is intended to be a companion book to remind you about God's power to recover all things.

First you must bind the strong man. First you must plunder his house. The strong man has already been plundered by the power of the Holy Spirit, but you need to go in and take back your goods now in the name of the Lord.

Through the wisdom of the Holy Spirit, pray through each one of the 12 recovery points and decide what you will recover today and then tomorrow and then next week. Within the next few months expect to see some goods recovered and some restoration happening. May the Lord seal the words of this chapter to your spirit and give you faith to activate them in your present circumstance. I look forward to hearing about all that you have recovered as you boldly bind the strong man and plunder his goods.

NOTES

1   Myron S. Augusburger, *The Communicator's Commentary: Matthew* (Waco, Tex.: Word Books, 1982), p. 157.

2   Elizabeth Alves, Barbara Femrite and Karen Kaufman, *Intercessors, Discover Your Prayer Power* (Ventura, Calif.: Regal Books, 2000), pp. 33-34.

3   The Voice of the Martyrs, *Jesus Freaks* (Albury Publishing, P.O. Box 470406 Tulsa, OK 74147-0406, 1999), pp. 208-209.

First the Greatest Commandment
Aligning Your Heart with God's

> "You must love the Lord your God with all your heart, all your soul, and all your mind. This is the first and greatest commandment."
> —Matthew 22:37,38 (NLT)

The context of this commandment is quoted in Matthew 22:34-40:

> But when the Pharisees heard that he had silenced the Sadducees with his reply, they thought up a fresh question of their own to ask him. One of them, an expert in religious law, tried to trap him with this question: "Teacher, which is the most important commandment in the law of Moses?" Jesus replied, "'You must love the Lord your God with all your heart, all your soul, and all your mind.' This is the first and greatest commandment" (NLT).

The question asked by the law expert was one that could be expected from him and from the men he represented. The scribes and Pharisees were devoted to carrying on lengthy debate about the commandments, arguing whether any particular one was great or small, heavy or light. It was natural, therefore, that they often debated the question as to which of the 613 commandments was the greatest. In this passage, they are asking about the greatest one. To this question,

Jesus gives His unforgettably beautiful reply. Quoting the Old Testament, He teaches that the whole duty of humanity, the whole moral spiritual law can be summed up in one word: love.

Love should first be directed to God. This commandment is first in time, first in rank, the most important. This is the greatest commandment upon which all other commandments will hang. Deuteronomy 6:5–"You shall love the LORD your God with all your heart, with all your soul, with all your strength"–was to be quoted twice daily by faithful Jews. The Jews were to unreservedly love God with every faculty of their personalities.

In John 14:15–"If you love Me, keep My commandments"–Jesus is simply saying that if you love God, you will automatically begin to keep all the other commandments. In 1 John 4:8 we read, "He who does not love does not know God, for God is love." Because God is the source and origin of love, all true love derives from God. God is love in His innermost being, and if we are to love, we must draw from His love first. Love for God should be the focus of our lives.

William H. Hinson illustrates the importance of focus by telling us why animal trainers carry a stool when they go into a cage of lions. They have their whips, of course, and their pistols are at their sides. But invariably they also carry a stool. Hinson says the stool is the trainer's most important tool. He holds the stool by the back and thrusts the legs toward the face of the wild animal. Those who know maintain that the animal tries to focus on all four legs at once. In the attempt to focus on all four things at once, a kind of paralysis overwhelms the animal, and it becomes tame, weak and disabled because its attention is fragmented.[1]

Much like the lion, we are often so paralyzed by second-rate loves that we can't focus on the main thing, which is to love God first and foremost. In the First Commandment, Jesus is simply taking the stool out of the hand of the world, so to speak, and encouraging us not to be fragmented in our hearts by focusing on too many things at one time. He wants us to understand that our love for Him should produce the overflow of every other action in our lives.

"Jesus quoted the very familiar passages of Scripture (see Deut. 6:5, Lev. 19:18), which summarize the whole Law in two basic principles:

Love God with all of your heart and out of that love will flow a love for people. Deuteronomy 6:5 is part of the Shema (Hebrew, 'hear'), the confession of faith of later Judaism that every adult male was obligated to recite each morning and evening. The Shema first points to God and affirms His unity and uniqueness. As the Lord (Yahweh, a personal name), He is the God who is the covenant keeper and who has revealed Himself in great deliverance. He has demonstrated His care and love, and He deserves the believers' love. As God (Elohim, from a root word which indicates 'majesty' and 'power'), He is all-powerful, and His followers can afford to trust themselves to Him in faith and love." [2]

"The Jews made many distinctions about the commandments of God, calling some 'light,' others 'weighty,' others 'little,' others 'great.' According to their estimating, some commandment must be greatest. Some of them contended that the law of the Sabbath was the greatest commandment, some the law of sacrifice, some that of circumcision and some pleaded for the wearing of phylacteries. They finally referred the resolution of this vexed question to Jesus, who astonished them by giving precedence to love." [3]

"Judaism taught that there were 613 commandments in the Law, one for each of the letters in the Ten Commandments. These 613 commandments consisted of 248 positive commands and 365 negative commands. The positive and negative commands were subdivided into major and lesser commands, i.e., more and less important. This division also involved a judgment based on how hard the command was to obey. Which was the greatest, they wanted to know." [4] The Jews had 613 commandments and now they wanted Jesus to tell them just which one was to be the first one, the most important one, the most fundamental one, the greatest. Jesus directed them back to love for God.

FOUR DESCRIPTIONS OF GOD IN SCRIPTURE

There are four descriptions of God in Scripture:

1. **God is Spirit.** John 4:24: "God is Spirit, and those who worship Him must worship in spirit and truth."

2. **God is light.** 1 John 1:5: This is the message which we have heard from Him and declare to you, that God is light and in Him is no darkness at all.

3. **God is fire.** Hebrews 12:29: For our God is a consuming fire.

4. **God is love.** 1 John 4:8: He who does not love does not know God, for Go is love.

God is love. He who is love is also light and fire. Far from condoning sin, His love has found a way to expose it—because He is light—and to consume it—because He is fire—yet, He does so by saving the sinner rather than by destroying the sinner. The capacity to love, whether the object of our love be God or our neighbors, is due entirely to His prior love for us and His love in us. First John 4:18,19 explains that "there is no fear in love; but perfect love casts out fear, because fear involves torment. But he who fears has not been made perfect in love. We love Him because He first loved us." God's love is primary.

THE FIRST COMMANDMENT, A PASSION COMMANDMENT

The first commandment is a passion commandment. We are not only told to love but we are also told to love passionately, with all of our being. The word "passion" actually refers to love, fervor and/or intensity, emotion, excitement, to be extremely excited, to stir or warm the blood, awaken energies, set on fire, stirred up, touch a chord, go to one's heart, touch to the quick, turn one's head, sweep off one's feet. Passion is the opposite of passive which is inactive, untouched, unemotional, unstirred, indifferent, neutrality, sluggishness.

*Passion is what motivates people to action. For example, I once heard a funny story about an attorney who moved to an eastern city which was so compacted that he decided to give up his car and walk to work. Late

> *"Passion is what motivates people to action."*

one evening, the attorney noticed a shortcut through a graveyard and decided to give it a try. He briskly moved along, that is, until he stumbled and fell into a deep pit. With no way out, the attorney stretched out his jacket and bedded down for the night. After midnight, the town drunk was meandering along and stumbled into the same pit. Startled, the attorney called out, "Hey! You can't get out of here so..." But the drunk did! You should have seen him move! At that moment, the drunk was so passionate about living that he was motivated right into sobriety. Passion will always result in emotion and action.

When you become passionate, you are easily moved in your emotions and in your spirit. You can be moved to love or moved to anger, easily excited or agitated by injury or emotion. You can have passionate affections, passionate desires and passionate concerns.

The biblical synonym for passion is "fervency," which means keeping up the boiling point by the spirit (see Rom. 12:11). It is keeping one's heart stirred up (see Exod. 35:21,26), and being baptized with the Holy Spirit and fire (see Matt. 3:1). Being stirred up is having hot desire. In 2 Timothy 1:6 we are told to stir up our gifts, meaning that we are to be passionate about them, fervernt in using them. We are to keep alive the flame of God's graciousness in us and to fan the flame of that special grace so that we might be used in the kingdom of God. To be passionate means that we are to be awakened and excited (see Isa. 51:9)—not allowing ourselves to become lukewarm (see Rev. 3:16).

THE COMMANDMENT IS TO LOVE GOD

The following story told by TimHansel explains how we "cab serve" God and yet fail to keep the commandment to love God.

A seminary professor set up his preaching class in an unusual way. He scheduled his students to preach on the "Parable of the Good Samaritan," and on the day of the class, he choreographed his experiment so that each student would go, one at a time, from one classroom to another where he or she would preach a sermon. The professor gave some students ten minutes to go from one room to the other; to others he allowed less time, forcing them to rush in order to meet the schedule. Each student, one at a time, had to walk down a certain corridor, passing by a bum who was deliberately planted there, obviously in need of some sort of aid. The results were surprising, and offered a powerful lesson.

The percentage of those good men and women who stopped to help was extremely low, expecially for those who were under the pressure of a shorter time period. The tighter the schedule, the fewer were those who stopped to help the indigent man. When the professor revealed his experiment, you can imagine the impact on that class of future spiritual leaders. Rushing to preach a sermon on the Good Samaritan, they had walked past the beggar at the heart of the parable! We must have eyes to see as well as hands to help, or we may never help at all. I think this well-known poem expresses it powerfully:

I was hungry and you formed a humanities club
to discuss my hunger.
Thank you.
I was imprisoned and you crept off quietly
to your chapel to pray for my release.
Nice.
I was naked and in your mind you debated
the morality of my appearance.
What good did that do?
I was sick and you knelt and thanked God for your health.
But I needed you.
I was homeless and you preached to me of the shelter
of the love of God.
I wish you'd taken me home.
I was lonely and you left me alone to pray for me.
Why didn't you stay?
You seem so holy, so close to God; but I'm still
very hungry, lonely, cold, and still in pain.
Does it matter?
(Anonymous) [5]

The antithesis of this story and poem was demonstrated through the life of Mother Teresa, who was so motivated to demonstrate her love for God that she loved all the hurting people in her world as though each one was Christ. She had a passion for God that was translated into action. No sacrifice was too costly for the man she called her Husband, the Lord Jesus Christ.

Real love forgets self. It doesn't count the cost. The Bible says, "Many waters cannot quench love, neither can the floods drown it." Our first commandment is simply to love God with fervency, stirring our hearts and having a passion for Him.

Jesus wants us to have a passionate kind of love—a love based on commitment and sacrifice. When Jesus commands us to love God with "all," He means love with a heart that is so fervent and so alive toward God that you would do anything for Him. Christ demonstrated His passion for us by dying on the cross and then giving us the Holy Spirit so that we would never suffer the pain of separation from Him again.

On May 2, 1962, a dramatic advertisement appeared in *The San Francisco Examiner*. "I don't want my husband to die in the gas chamber for a crime he did not commit. I will, therefore, offer my services for 10 years as a cook, maid, or housekeeper to any leading attorney who will defend him and bring about his vindication." One of San Francisco's greatest attorneys, Vincent Hallinan, read or heard about the ad and contacted Gladys Kidd, the woman who had placed it. Her husband, Robert Lee Kidd, was about to be tried for the slaying of an elderly antique dealer. Kidd's fingerprints had been found on a bloodstained ornate sword in the victim's shop. During the trial, Hallinan proved that the antique dealer had not been killed by the sword, and that Kidd's fingerprints and blood on the sword got there because Kidd had once toyed with it while playfully dueling with a friend when they were both out shopping. The jury, after 11 hours, found Kidd to be not guilty. Attorney Hallinan refused Gladys Kidd's offer of 10 years of servitude.[6]

He could not allow such love to be punished by servitude; that kind of love deserved to be rewarded and recognized. Though Hallinan set Gladys free from her commitment to pay the debt, she willing would have given 10 years of her life because of her covenantal love for her husband. Gladys understood the meaning of loving with "all" of her heart.

THE GREEK WORDS FOR LOVE

In the Greek language used at the time of the New Testament there were three main words used to describe what the English language has only one word for: "love." The word *phileo* refers to love in a general sense, care, friendship that exists between family members and friends, a general attraction towards a person or thing, devotion, affection. It refers to brotherly love. The city of Philedelphia gets its name after *phileo* kind of love.

The word *eros* (which is not used in the New Testament) means love that desires to take possession, a craving, desire. The Greeks delighted in bodily beauty and sensual desires, sensual ecstasy describes the irresistible power of sensual love, which they personified in the Greek god of love, Eros. *Eros* is a love that forgets all reason, will and discretion on the way to ecstasy in fulfilling cravings; it desires to take possession of something.

Third is the word *agape*. A love of the will, a love directed by decision and commitment, a love that wills to initiate a relationship and show kindness and self-sacrifice, regardless of whether the object of love is worthy or even likeable. Thus, *agape* is a love that does not depend on an emotional response, rather it is an expression of the nature and character of the one who loves.

Throughout the Scriptures, the word *agape* is used when Jesus speaks about His love for His people, His love for God and how we should love God and our brothers and sisters in Christ. The first commandment is to *agape* God, not *phileo* or *eros* Him. The command to love the Lord with all one's heart can only be undertaken in response to His own love. The ability to love with this capacity is realized only because He extended His love first. *Agape* is not demonstrated by sentimental goo, or lip service; *agape* is a love characterized by will, sacrifice and action as it reaches out toward its object in mercy and grace. *Agape* is an unconditional love that burns intensely as it reflects the love of the Cross, a love of sacrifice.

In order to know how to love God, we must understand that God is love. His nature is love. God's love is among the most difficult concepts to grasp. We don't understand the love of God. We don't understand that God loves us all the time, in every circumstance. Our moods do not at all infringe on the mood of God, because God does not have moods that change with regard to love. He loves us at all times, whether we do good or bad. When have a hard time accepting love, we have a hard time giving love. We must understand that God is love. His love drew us to Him and captivated our hearts. His love keeps us. His love feeds us. His love satisfies us (see 1 John 4:8; 4:16; 2 Cor. 13:11).

FOUR CHARACTERISTICS OF GOD'S LOVE

The following are four main characteristics of God's love that He Himself possesses and wants to pass on to us as we love Him.

1. Benevolence

Benevolence is the basic dimension of God's love. By benevolence, we mean the concern that God has for the welfare of those whom He loves as He watches out for us at all times (see Deut. 7:7,8).

Benevolent love is self-giving goodness. This unselfish quality of divine love is seen in what God has done. God sent Jesus to redeem us. God sent Jesus to die for us. God sent Jesus so that He could take care of us and watch over us and deal with our sins, even while we were His enemies.

In *The Grace of Giving,* Stephen Olford tells about a Baptist pastor during the American Revolution, Peter Miller, who lived in Ephrata, Pennsylvania, and enjoyed the friendship of George Washington.

In Ephrata also lived Michael Wittman, an evil-minded sort who did all he could to oppose and humiliate the pastor.

One day Michael Wittman was arrested for treason and sentenced to die. Peter Miller traveled seventy miles on foot to Philadelphia to plead for the life of the traitor.

"No, Peter," General Washington said, "I cannot grant you the life of your friend."

"My friend!" exclaimed the old preacher. "He's the bitterest enemy I have."

93

"What?" cried Washington. "You've walked seventy miles to save the life of an enemy? That puts the matter in a different light. I'll grant your pardon." And he did. Peter Miller took Michael Wittman back home to Ephrata—no longer an enemy, but a friend.[7]

Peter Miller walked 70 miles to benevolently save the life of an undeserving man. But Jesus Christ walked into the hell of rejection and even death for you and for me to make us His friends. He is the sourse of all that is benevolent.

> Roman 5:10: For if when we were enemies we were reconciled to God through the death of His Son, much more, having been reconciled, we shall be saved by His life.
> 1 John 4:10: In this is love, not that we loved God, but that He loved us and sent His Son to be the propitiation for our sins.

2. Grace

God deals with us not on the basis of our merit or worthiness or on what we deserve, but simply according to our need. In other words, He deals with us on the basis of His goodness and generosity. Grace means that God supplies us with undeserved favors. He requires nothing from us. It is His nature to be gracious to us (see Exod. 34:6). Someone once said, "Grace means that while we were sinners and enemies, we have been treated as sons and heirs."

As a shepherd was tending his sheep, two wolves attacked. One of the wolves killed the mother of one of the youngest lambs; the other wolf killed a small lamb as its mother looked on helplessly.

The shepherd finally succeeded in driving the wolves away, but he was left with a delimena. He had lost one mother and one small lamb. Now, he was in danger of losing a second lamb because its mother had been killed and none of the other sheep would nurse the lamb since it was not their own. Then the shepherd came up with a plan.

He took the skin of the dead lamb and put it over the live lamb. In doing this, he caused the grieving mother to recognize the orphaned lamb as her own. So the mother accepted the little lamb, nursed it and it became her own.[8]

When Jesus went to the cross for our sins, He laid His coat of righteousness over our unrighteous so that we are now clothed in Christ (see Gal. 3:26,27). All the gifts of heaven are your inheritance as a son or daughter of the Lord, and He longs to bless you.

Ephesians 1:5-8 says it in the following words:

Having predestined us to adoption as sons by Jesus Christ to Himself, according to the good pleasure of His will, to the praise of the glory of His grace, by which He has made us accepted in the Beloved. In Him we have redemption through His blood, the forgiveness of sins, according to the riches of His grace which He made to abound toward us in all wisdom and prudence.

We are accepted in the beloved because of the cross of Christ and the love of God. We can't do anything to earn God's acceptance—it is a gift of grace which is freely given so that we might enjoy the goodness of God (see Titus 3:4-7).

3 Mercy

God's mercy is seen in His tenderhearted, loving compassion. James 2:13 says that "mercy triumphs over judgment." God does not judge us for our wrongs according to what we deserve; He hears our cries and has compassion on us. He judges us as sinners by the Cross. He understands our failures, our stumblings, our poor decisions and our character flaws, and pours His mercy upon us when we least deserve it. His tender mercies toward us are so great that we often have a hard time receiving them.

God is faithful toward us. He doesn't cast us away if we fail, fall short or make mistakes. He loves us continually, in spite of our sins and failure. David failed and God not only forgave David but stayed by his side. Moses failed. Abraham made some serious mistakes. You have failed and so have I. But God's mercy covers His children.

The parable of the prodigal son gives us a snapshot of God's mercy and love for us: a father's response to a broken person (see Luke 15). The prodigal had squandered his life on things the father could not bless. Yet the father met him, actually ran out to meet him, kissed him and restored him and clothed him with a new robe and shoes, bestowing on him the father's ring. The father could have judged his son, putting him down and putting him out. But he didn't. Instead, he lifted him up and loved him back into the family. Thank God that He withholds judgment and offers mercy to us rather than what we deserve.

> Psalm 103:13: As a father pities his children, so the LORD pities those who fear Him.
> Mark 1:41: And Jesus, moved with compassion, put out His hand and touched him, and said to him, "I am willing; be cleansed."

> Jesus shows mercy toward suffering, sick, tormented and helpless people.

> Matthew 9:35,36: Then Jesus went about all the cities and villages, teaching in their synagogues, preaching the gospel of the kingdom, and healing every sickness and every disease among the people. But when He saw the multitudes, He was moved with compassion for them, because they were weary and scattered, like sheep having no shepherd.

4. Persistence

The fourth characteristic of God's love is persistence. As we've just discovered, God withholds judgment and continues to offer benevolence, grace and mercy over long periods of time. God doesn't abandon us or get frustrated with us. He is persistent about showing His love to us.

Remember the story of Humpty Dumpty?

Humpty Dumpty sat on the wall.
Humpty Dumpty had a great fall.
All the King's horses and all the King's men
Couldn't put Humpty together again.

As we understand and respond to the persistent love of God, our capacity to love should change. The following story by Vic Pentz of "Humpty Dumpty Revisited" illustrates how the persistent love of God for broken people can bring about wholeness and change.

But soon the King himself heard of Humpty's fate....The King meandered through the back streets and alleys in search of Humpty. After several days and nights the persistent monarch found him. Humpty's shattered body was scattered over a ten-foot circle amidst the broken glass and flattened beer cans of a back alley.

Though weak from his searching, the King was overjoyed at the sight of Humpty. He ran to his side and cried, "Humpty! It is I your King! I have powers greater than those of my horses and men who failed to put you together again. Be at peace. I am here to help!"

"Leave me alone," Humpty's mouth retorted. "I've gotten used to this new way of life. I kind of like it now."

"But—" was all the King could get out before Humpty continued.

"I tell you, I'm fine. I like it here....

The King tried again. "I assure you my kingdom has much more to offer than this back alley—there are green mountains, rolling surfs, exciting cities...."

But Humpty would hear none of it. And the saddened King returned to the palace.

A week later one of Humpty's eyes rolled skyward only to see once again the concerned face of the King standing over his fractured pieces.

"I've come to help," firmly stated the King.

"Look, leave me alone, will you!" said Humpty. "I've just

seen my psychiatrist, and he assures me that I'm doing a fine job of coping with my environment as it is. You're a cop-out. A man has to deal with life as it comes. I'm a realist."

"But wouldn't you rather walk?" asked the King.

"Look," Humpty's mouth replied, "once I get up and start walking, I'll have to stay up and keep walking. At this point in my life I'm not ready to make a commitment like that. So, if you'll excuse me—you're blocking my sun."

Reluctantly, the King turned once again and walked through the streets of his kingdom back to the palace.

It was over a year before the King ventured to return to Humpty's side. But sure enough, one bright morning one of Humpty's ears perked up at the sure, steady stride of the King. This time he was ready. Humpty's eye turned toward the tall figure just as his mouth managed the words, "My King!"

Immediately the King fell to his knees on the glass-covered pavement. His strong, knowing hands gently began to piece together Humpty's fragments. After some time, his work completed, the King rose to full height, pulling up with him the figure of a strong man.

The two walked hand in hand throughout the kingdom. Together they stood atop lush green mountains. They ran together along deserted beaches. They laughed and joked together as they strolled the gleaming cities of the King's domain. This went on forever. And to the depth, breadth, and height of their friendship there was no end.

Once, while walking together down the sidewalk in one of the King's cities, Humpty overheard a remark that made his heart leap with both the joy of his new life and the bitter memory of the back alley. Someone said, "Say, who are those two men?"

Another replied, "Why the one on the left is old Humpty Dumpty. I don't know the one on the right—but they sure look like brothers!"[9]

THE POWER OF LOVE

Like Humpty Dumpty, we have a capacity to actually move our passions toward God and release our love to Him. God created us with a capacity to love, and we need to use this love properly (see Ps. 18:1; John 15:13; Rom. 5:5).

> *"God created us with a capacity to love, and we need to use this love properly."*

We are to love the Lord our God with all of our hearts, souls and our minds. "The word 'all' speaks of total submission and dedication; it excludes any half-heartedness. The heart is the seat of the emotions, in general, and of love in particular. The soul is the center of the personality; loving with one's soul thus implies that love must permeate the core of an individual's being, to his or her very will. Deuteronomy 6:5 does not mention the mind separately, but the Hebrew for 'heart' does include the mind, so Jesus drew attention to it. The mind is important in loving 'in truth,' that is, in full agreement with the revealed will of God. 'These words' in Deuteronomy 6:6 refers to the Ten Commandments. Israel was to love God first before they could even begin to keep the commandments."[11]

MISDIRECTED LOVE

God allows us to direct our love. Some people love funny things and some love different things: hobbies, animals, jobs, collecting little things, sports. Some people love themselves more than anything else.

First, we can have a misdirected love for things that are good or morally neutral. C. S. Lewis talks about how a mother's love for her kids, if allowed to replace her love for God, can become suffocatingly protective and even demonic. We can also love those things that God does not want us to love and things that will hinder us from having a fulfilling and profitable life for Christ. We can misdirect our love into loving money more than God:

Psalm 62:10: Do not trust in oppression, nor vainly hope in robbery; if riches increase, do not set your heart on them.

1 Timothy 6:10: For the love of money is a root of all kinds of evil, for which some have strayed from the faith in their greediness, and pierced themselves through with many sorrows.

We are not to allow our pursuit of money or material things to supersede our love for God. Although Scripture does say that God wants us to prosper and enjoy the riches of life, we are not to set our hearts on them and love them above God.

Misdirected love can also love evil things, those things that are carnal and wrong. We are not to love things that are evil:

Psalm 78:8: And may not be like their fathers, a stubborn and rebellious generation, a generation that did not set its heart aright, and whose spirit was not faithful to God.

Ecclesiastes 8:11: Because the sentence against an evil work is not executed speedily, therefore, the heart of the sons of men is fully set in them to do evil.

Hosea 4:8: They eat up the sin of My people; they set their heart on their iniquity.

We are not to love money; we are not to love evil; we are not to love human wisdom:

Ecclesiastes 1:17: And I set my heart to know wisdom and to know madness and folly. I perceived that this also is grasping for the wind.

1 Corinthians 1:19-25: For it is written: "I will destroy the wisdom of the wise, and bring to nothing the understanding of the prudent." Where is the wise? Where is the scribe? Where is the disputer of this age? Has not God made foolish the wisdom of this world? For since, in the wisdom of God, the world through wisdom did not know God, it pleased God through the foolishness of the message preached to save those who believe. For Jews request a

sign, and Greeks seek after wisdom; but we preach Christ crucified, to the Jews a stumbling block and to the Greeks foolishness, but to those who are called, both Jews and Greeks, Christ the power of God and the wisdom of God. Because the foolishness of God is wiser than men, and the weakness of God is stronger than men.

We are also not to love the world:

> 1 John 2:15: Do not love the world or the things in the world. If anyone loves the world, the love of the Father is not in him.

GOD-DIRECTED LOVE

We need to develop a God-directed love. We need to develop the discipline to direct our hearts toward those things that God blesses and God lifts up. We are to obey the first commandment. We are to first, above everything else, love the Lord our God, which means we must love the things He loves. A God-directed love is a love that the person has decided to harness and direct toward the right areas.

- We are to love to seek the Lord through prayer (see 1 Chron. 22:19).
- We are to love the house of the Lord (see 2 Chron. 24:4).
- We are to love pursuing and following God (see Ps. 84:5)
- We are to love the Lord Jesus Christ (see Eph. 6:24)
- We are to love the Holy Spirit (see Col. 1:8).
- We are to love one another (see 1 Pet. 1:22; 2:17).
- We are to love God's commandments (see Ps. 119:127,165).
- We are to love God's name (see Ps. 119:132).
- We are to love salvation (see Ps. 70:4).

We have the potential to corrupt our love, but we also have the potential to direct our love. F. B. Meyer said, "This was Adam's blessed privilege in Eden; but he missed it. The love of self took the place of the love of God. It is the aim of our blessed Lord to bring us back to that position."[12] We can be corrupted by the world. Our love can be corrupted by the spirit of this world. We can be corrupted by the flesh. Our flesh has the power to seduce us, twist our desires and corrupt our purity. We can be corrupted by the devil. Our love is a prize for the devil to capture. He will do anything to draw our love away from God.

REVIVING OUR PASSIONS FOR GOD

Count Zinzendorf said, "I have but one passion; it is He, He only." We need to revive our passions for God. Reviving our passion for God will come through cleansing.

Cleanse Your Heart

We need to cleanse our hearts. Deuteronomy 30:6 says, "The LORD your God will circumcise your heart and the heart of your descendants, to love the LORD your God with all your heart and with all your soul, that you may live." And 2 Chronicles 34:27 reads, "Because your heart was tender, and you humbled yourself before God when you heard His words against this place and against its inhabitants, and you humbled yourself before Me, and you tore your clothes and wept before Me, I also have heard you, says the LORD." Of course, Psalm 51:10 is one of those famous Scriptures that we should all pray on a daily basis:

> Create in me a clean heart, O God, and renew a steadfast spirit within me.

Psalm 66:18 says, "If I regard iniquity in my heart, the Lord will not hear." The very first step to restoring your passion for God is to restore your heart. Restoring your heart calls for repentance, asking the Holy Spirit to come and cleanse, applying the blood of Christ in a very practical way to the stubborn habits of the flesh and carnal mind.

Cleanse Your Emotions

We must also cleanse our emotions. Emotions can be corrupted and twisted by the world, the flesh, the devil and many of our carnal decisions that allow our emotions to be hindered or twisted into feelings and habits that are not acceptable to God. The Bible tells us that our emotions can be changed. They can be ruled; they can also be controlled. Proverbs 25:28 says, "Whoever has no rule over his own spirit (that is, his own emotions) is like a city broken down (that is, his life is open for devastation), without walls (that is, he has no protection)." We are encouraged throughout Scripture to take our emotions and to rule them and to cleanse them.

Emotions can be changed. Psalm 42:11 says, "Why are you cast down, O my soul? And why are you disquieted?" You and I might think, *There is no help here for my emotions.* Yet Psalm 42:11 says we are to discipline ourselves and say to our emotions, "Hope in God; for I shall yet praise Him, the help of my countenance and my God."

Our emotions can be aligned and changed by faith. Second Corinthians 5:7 simply says, "For we walk by faith, not by sight." Or we could say we walk by faith and not by emotions. We are to change our emotions and align our emotions with the Word of God by faith. Our emotions can be focused on the right things. We do not need to allow misdirected love or misdirected emotions. Matthew 22:37 tells us to "love the LORD your God with all your heart, with all your soul, and with all your mind." This means we direct our emotions toward God, fasten our emotions upon God and discipline our emotions to love God.

Our emotions can be Holy Spirit empowered. Galatians 5:22 says, "But the fruit of the Spirit is love, joy, peace, longsuffering, kindness, goodness, faithfulness." We know that as the Spirit grows in us, our emotions can be harnessed by the Holy Spirit and the fruit of the Holy Spirit will be evidenced in our lives.

Cleanse Your Mind

We must also cleanse our minds. If we are to direct our love, we must start with a clean mind. Psalm 26:2 says, "Examine me, O LORD, and prove me; try my mind and my heart." Psalm 66:10 says, "For You, O God, have tested us; You have refined us as silver is refined." We know that we are to take our thoughts and have them cleansed before the Lord. A wandering thought during prayer time, worship time or daily living can cause misdirected love if allowed to reign in the mind. We are to love the Lord with all of our hearts; we are also to love Him with all of our thoughts. We can say we love the Lord with our minds, and our thoughts can run wild. Discipline comes one thought at a time, one minute a day, every hour. We are to love the Lord God with our thoughts.

"Give your mind, your will, your power of choice to God. Make Him first. Ask Him to take the helm of your life, and to control, inspire and direct its every movement. Crown Him King. And when the will...has puts its crown of life on the head of Christ...all the emotions and affections and faculties of heart and life will come in to swell the court with their homage and acclaim."[13] (See Deuteronomy 30:20; Joshua 22:5; Judges 20:45; Psalm 63:8; 2 Chronicles 15:12.)

Let us be like the psalmist who proclaimed, "When You said, 'Seek My face,' my heart said to You, 'Your face, Lord, I will seek.'" That kind of seeking will require all your heart, all your soul and all your mind.

Return to your first love and make love your first thing.

NOTES

1   John Maxwell, *Developing the Leader Within You* (Nashville:Thomas Nelson, 1993), p. 31.

2   Ralph W. Harris, ed., *The New Testament Study Bible*, Matthew (Springfield, Mo.: The Complete Library, 1989), p. 485.

3   Spence, H.D.M. ed., *The Pulpit Commentary: Volume 15, Matthew* (Grand Rapids: Eerdmans, 1978), p. 387.

4   Ralph W. Harris, ed., *The New Testament Study Bible, Matthew*, ibid.

5   Alice Gray, ed., *Stories for the Heart*, "The Good Samaritan" by Tim Hansel (Sisters, Oreg.; Multnomah: 1996), pp. 87-88.

6   From *The Book of Lists #2*, p. 157.
http://www.christianglobe.com/Illustrations/a-z/l/love_example_of.htm

7   Craig Brian Larson, ed., *Illustrations for Preaching & Teaching* (Co-published by Christianity Today, Inc., and Baker Book House Company, 1993), p.131.

8   Jim Burns and Greg McKinnon, *Illustrations, Stories and Quotes* (Ventura, Calif.: Gospel Light, 1997), p. 51.

9   Alice Gray, ed., *Stories for the Heart*, "Humpty Dumpty Revisited" by Vic Pentz, pp. 28-30.

10 Myron S. Augsburger, *The Communicator's Commentary: Matthew* (Waco, Tex.: Word Books, 1982), p. 258.

11 Ralph W. Harris, ed., *The New Testament Study Bible Matthew* (Springfield, Mo.: The Complete Library, 1989), p. 485.

12 F.B. Meyer, *Great Verses Through the Bible* (Grand Rapids, Mich.: Zondervan Publishing, 1966), p. 376.

13 F. B. Meyer, *Great Verses Through the Bible* (Grand Rapids: Zondervan Publishing, 1966), p. 377.

First Cleanse the Inside
Aligning Your Inner World

"First cleanse the inside of the cup and dish,
that the outside of them may be clean also."
—Matthew 23:26

Ralph Waldo Emerson said that "the gods we worship write their names on our faces." The inside will always affect the outward, and our God is the God of the inside and the outside. Therefore, the inward experience of salvation is the beginning of a change that eventually becomes outward change.

She was an embittered woman, Charlotte Elliott of Brighton, England. Her health was broken, and her disability had hardened her. "If God loved me," she muttered, "He would not have treated me this way."

Hoping to help her, a Swiss minister named Dr. Cesar Malan visited the Elliotts on May 9. 1822. Over dinner, Charlotte lost her temper and railed against God and family in a violent outburst. Her embarrassed family left the room, and Dr. Malan, left alone with her, stared at her across the table.

"You are tired of yourself, aren't you?" he said at length. "You are holding to your hate and anger because you have nothing else in the world to cling to. Consequently, you have become sour, bitter, and resentful."

"What is your cure?" asked Charlotte.

"The faith you are trying to despise."

As they talked, Charlotte softened. "If I wanted to become a Christian and to share the peace and joy you possess," she finally asked, "what would I do?"

"You would give yourself to God just as you are now, with your fightings, fears, hates and loves, pride and shame."

"I would come to God just as I am? Is that right?"

Charlotte did come just as she was. Her heart was changed that day. As time passed, she found and claimed John 6:37 as a special verse for her: "...the one who comes to Me I will by no means cast out."

Several years later, her brother, Rev. Henry Elliott, was raising funds for a school for the children of poor clergymen. Charlotte wrote a poem, and it was printed and sold across England. The leaflet said: *Sold For the Benefit of St. Margaret's Hall, Brighton: Him That Cometh To Me I Will In No Wise Cast Out.* Underneath was Charlotte's poem—which has since become the most famous invitational hymn in history:

> Just as I am, without one plea,
> But that Thy blood was shed for me,
> And that Thou bidd'st me come to Thee,
> O Lamb of God, I come! I come! [1]

YOUR LIFE, GOD'S TABERNACLE

Scripture reveals God as being exceedingly interested in what He made—not only outwardly but also inwardly. The Old Testament Tabernacle of Moses, the place of worship for the people of Israel, is an example of the emphasis God puts on inner beauty as opposed to mere outward beauty. The outer appearance of the Tabernacle of Moses was not eye-appealing; it was made of badger skin. In stark contrast, the inside of the Tabernacle was decorated with intricately woven veils and lovely tapestries. The Tabernacle is symbolic of the Holy Spirit's continuous weaving together of beautiful qualities in our character as He brings our lives into Kingdom alignment.

Exodus 25:11 describes the ark of the covenant, the place where God's presence dwelt and God's voice was heard:

> "And you shall overlay it with pure gold, inside and out you shall overlay it, and shall make on it a molding of gold all around."

As with every piece of furniture in the Tabernacle of Moses, Moses was given specific instructions for building this piece of furniture. I want you to notice the words in Exodus 25:11:

> "It shall be pure gold, inside and out."

The Holy Spirit not only wants to overlay us with gold, but He also wants to inlay us with pure gold. Even in places people cannot see, there should be intricate weavings of God's character, which is purified gold, reproduced in us.

THE KINGDOM OF THE UPSIDE DOWN

God's Kingdom is the kingdom of the upside down. "To live, you must die. To be chief, you must serve. To be exalted, you must be abased. To be whole, you must be broken. The world sees from the outside in; Jesus sees from the inside out. So there's no doubt, if in him I can hide, there Christ will abide. In my heart, that's where he starts in the kingdom of the inside out and the upside down" (*J.B. Phillips*).

In Matthew 23, Jesus describes the Kingdom of the upside down—one of the strongest chapters in the New Testament concerning the pronouncements of Christ's judgment upon the Pharisees and the religious system of His day. Matthew 23:25-28 will be our key text as we delve into first cleansing the inside, renouncing destructive sins.

"Woe to you, scribes and Pharisees, hypocrites! For you cleanse the outside of the cup and dish, but inside they are full of extortion and self-indulgence. Blind Pharisee, first cleanse the inside of the cup and dish, that the outside of them may be clean also. Woe to you, scribes and Pharisees, hypocrites! For you are like whitewashed tombs which indeed appear beautiful outwardly, but inside are full of dead men's bones and all uncleanness. Even so you also outwardly appear righteous to men, but inside you are full of hypocrisy and lawlessness."

Notice in these verses the words "outside" and "inside" and you will get a sense of what Jesus values and also what Jesus rebukes.

THE CONTEXT OF MATTHEW 23

To understand this first thing principle of "first cleanse the inside," we must understand the context in which Jesus spoke it. Matthew 23 is broken into three sections:

- Verses 1-12 describes the sins of the scribes and Pharisees.
- Verses 13-36 pronounces the woes upon them.
- Verses 37-39 describes Christ's love for Jerusalem.

Jesus encouraged His followers to obey the religious teachers as they taught the law of Moses, because the law of Moses was worthy of their reverence and obedience. But, more importantly, He also taught them not to follow the practice of the Pharisees. Jesus disqualified the leadership of the Pharisees by making several observations. He began by saying that they multiplied commands upon individuals which they themselves did not practice—in other words, He exposed their hypocrisy. He went on to say that they practiced their religious traditions to receive recognition from men—in other words, they were dominated by a man-pleasing spirit rather than a reverence for God. He also said they were respected because they had chief places in the assembly and that they sought to be greeted with honor in society—in other words, they were status seeks.

Jesus condemned their status seeking and contrasted their practice with the new community that He was creating. The new people of God have one teacher, Christ, and one level of honor. All are brethren with one Father before whom all bow, the Father in heaven. They have one measure of greatness, that of being servants who humble themselves in service. What a remarkable outline for worship and relationship within the Church for we who are called true disciples by Christ.

The seven woes Jesus proclaimed against the scribes and Pharisees are because:

1. They shut the door of the Kingdom in people's faces (v. 13).
2. They corrupted proselytes (v. 15).
3. They reversed the truth regarding the oath (v. 22).
4. They inverted values (vv. 23,24).
5. They elevated the importance of ritual (vv. 25,26).
6. They externalized religion (vv. 27,28)
7. They sought status by exalting themselves and their superior goodness (vv. 29-32).

The fifth and sixth woes pinpoint the scrupulous attention the Pharisees gave to the religious externals, a focus that led to a disregard of inner perversions. Jesus reveals their outward conformity of appearance to be seen by men that often concealed the inner corruption of moral defilement.

The Message translates our pilot passage, Matthew 23:25-28, as follows:

"You're hopeless, you religious scholars and Pharisees! Frauds! You burnish the surface of your cups and bowls so they sparkle in the sun, while the insides are maggoty with your greed and gluttony. Stupid Pharisee! Scour the insides, and then the gleaming surface will mean something. You're hopeless, you religious scholars and Pharisees! Frauds! You're like manicured grave plots, grass clipped and the flowers bright, but six feet down it's all rotting bones and worm-eaten flesh. People look at you and think you're saints, but beneath the skin you're total frauds."

Even today, Jesus penetrates the religious community with these fiery words that burn off the dross and the outward deceptions of religious traditions, revealing the true state of the heart. God wants to expose our inner fears, pride and self-protective places so that when we have been stripped of all self-effort, we will reflect the true righteousness of Christ. We are trees of righteousness, the planting of the Lord.

When a tree's life is threatened, stressed by the elements of fire, drought or other calamity, it twists beneath its bark to reinforce and make itself stronger. On the surface, this new inner strength may not be visible, for the bark often continues to give the same vertical appearance. Only when the exterior is stripped away, or when the tree is felled, are its inner struggles revealed.[2]

Like the tree just described, on the surface we can appear one way and yet be very different on the inside. Our inner character flaws as well as our inner character strengths may not be visible for all to see, but they are alive and well on the inside. We are not just interested in stripping away the exterior, but we are also interested in changing something inside—where real change actually begins. We need a new inner life.

INSIDE LIFE REQUIRES INSIDE CHRIST

If we are to have new life, we must have a new birth. Inside life requires that Christ lives inside us. Revelation 3:20 says, "Behold, I stand at the door and knock. If anyone hears My voice and opens the door, I will come in to him and dine with him, and he with Me." Inside change requires an inside change agent, which for us as Christians is the Holy Spirit, who brings into our lives the presence and power of a living Christ. First Corinthians 15:22 explains:

For as in Adam all die, even so in Christ all shall be made alive.

The following quote by E. Stanley Jones is one of the greatest classics of all times; it is called "In Christ." Jones is debating with the religious community about his missionary call to India and about the state of the lost soul of humankind, whether people are really lost to hell or not.

> There is a concept that reduces the whole of life to its utmost simplicity. If you have it, you are in. If you don't have it, you are out. By in, I mean "in life," and by out, "out of life." I felt I had found that concept in the phrase "in Christ." If you are in Christ, you are in life. If you are out of Christ, you are out of life. If that proposition be true, then it cuts down through all veneer, all seeming, all make-believe, all marginalisms, all halfwayisms, through everything and brings us to the ultimate essence of things. If you are in Christ, you are in life. If you out of Christ, you are out of life. Here now and here after. This concept goes deeper than being interested in religion, for you may be interested in religion and not be in Christ. You may be in the church and not be in Christ, in orthodoxy and not in Him, in the new birth and not in Christ. For the new birth may be in the past and only faintly operative now. You may be in conversion and not in Christ, for the conversion may have ceased to convert to Him. The phrase "in Christ" is the ultimate phrase in the Christian faith, for it locates us in a person, the divine person, and it locates us in Him, here and now. It brings us to the ultimate relationship–in. Obviously, this "in" brings us nearer than near Christ, following Christ, believing in Christ really being committed to Christ. You cannot go further or deeper than in.[3]

To have inside life, we must have inside Christ. Life requires a step of faith and a true conversion to Christ and a living in Christ. Ephesians 2:1 says, "And you He made alive, who were dead in trespasses and sins." We must understand that we have to pass from death to life.

New Inside Life Requires New Birth

In John 3:3 we find the requirement for new inside life:

Jesus answered and said to him, "Most assuredly, I say to you, unless one is born again, he cannot see the kingdom of God."

Perhaps you are wondering how this transformation from death to life happens. I can think of no one who describes the process better than Keith Phillips in his book *The Making of a Disciple*:

Let's suppose that on January 1, I was flying over Kansas when the plane exploded. My body fell to the ground and I was dead on impact. Before long a farmer discovered my corpse. There was no pulse, no heartbeat, no breath. My body was cold. Obviously, I was dead. So the farmer dug a grave. But by the time he placed my body in the earth, it was too dark to cover it. Deciding he would finish in the morning, he returned home.

Then Christ came to me and said, "Keith, you are dead. Your life on earth is over. But I will breathe into you a breadth of new life if you promise to do anything I ask and go anywhere I send you."

My immediate reaction was, "No way!" That's unreasonable. It's slavery." But then I realized I was not in a good bargaining position, and I quickly came to my senses. I wholeheartedly agreed.

Instantly, my lungs, heart and other vital organs began to function again. I came back to life. I was born again! From that point on, no matter what Christ asked me to do or where He asked me to go, I was more than willing. No task was too difficult, no hours too long, no place too dangerous. Nothing was unreasonable. Why? Because I had no claim to my life. I was living on borrowed time, Christ's time. Keith died on January 1 in a Kansas cornfield. Then I could say with Paul, "I have been crucified [have died] with Christ; and it is no longer [Keith] who is alive, but Christ [who] lives in me...."

That is what self-death and being born again are about. Christ's command to "Follow Me" is an injunction to participate in His death in order to experience new life. You become a living dead man, totally committed to Him.

Now let's look at what some other disciples of Christ have had to say about death to the old self and being born again:

- "The new birth is not only a mystery that no man understands. It is a miracle that no man undertakes..." (Richard Baxter)

- "We must first be made good before we can do good." (Hugh Latimer)

- "The spirit recreates the human heart, quickening it from spiritual death to spiritual life. Regenerate people are new creations. When formerly they had no disposition, inclination or desire for the things of God, now they are disposed and inclined toward God. In regeneration, new birth, God plants a desire for Himself in the human heart that otherwise would not be there." (R. C. Sproul)

- "A dead man cannot assist in his own resurrection. Had it not been for the gracious work of the Holy Spirit who gave us a new life complete with a new nature and a new desire to please, serve, obey and glorify God, we would be spiritually dead and hostile to God." (W. G. T. Shedd)

NEW INSIDE LIFE REQUIRES NEW IDENTITY

As we've just read, we move from death to life. We move from our old man to our new man. We move from our old ways to our new ways. That change begins on the inside and then moves to the operation behaviors of our lives. Old things pass away and all things become new. New inside life has a beginning point, a process and an ultimate end, which is to become like Christ. Second Corinthians 5:17 puts it this way:

Therefore, if anyone is in Christ, he is a new creation; old things have passed away; behold, all things have become new.

Thomas Adams said that "becoming a Christian is not making a new start in life. It is receiving a new life to start with." When we are born again, we have a new identity, which is clearly delineated in Scripture. The following verses explain:

Ephesians 2:10: For we are His workmanship, created in Christ Jesus for good works, which God prepared beforehand that we should walk in them.

1 Peter 2:9,10: But you are a chosen generation, a royal priest-hood, a holy nation, His own special people, that you may proclaim the praises of Him who called you out of darkness into His marvelous light; who once were not a people but are now the people of God, who had not obtained mercy but now have obtained mercy.

Romans 8:17: And if children, then heirs—heirs of God and joint heirs with Christ, if indeed we suffer with Him, that we may also be glorified together.

Galatians 4:6,7: And because you are sons, God has sent forth the Spirit of His Son into your hearts, crying out, "Abba, Father!" Therefore you are no longer a slave but a son, and if a son, then an heir of God through Christ.

While walking through the forest one day, a man found a young eagle that had fallen out of its nest. The man took the eaglet home, put it in his barnyard and raised it among his chickens. For several years the eagle acted like a chicken, ate like a chicken, lived like a chicken. Yet within the eagle was the nature of an eagle, a nature that could not be removed. Then one day the eagle left the chicken coop to soar among the clouds as it was born to do. His inside nature determined his outside behavior.

INSIDE CLEANING REQUIRES INSIDE WORK

We *have been* changed, we *are being* changed and we *shall be* totally changed. To change our wrong behaviors and carnal habits, we need to cleanse the inside and see the inner change become a reality through yieldedness to the enabling power of the Holy Spirit. Changing the inside begins by changing our thoughts. Our minds play a large part in the conversion process that we go through when we accept Christ. But to continue the process of change, we must reprogram our minds with the Word of God. Romans 10:17 says that "faith comes by hearing, and hearing by the word of God." As we plant the Word of God in our minds, it will take root and we will find ourselves saying what God says. We'll start to speak faith because the Word will germinate positive thoughts and faith thoughts in our minds. Believing you can live a victorious Christian life takes no more effort than believing you cannot. You simply chose between God's truth and Satan's lies. Hear the truth of the Lord:

> "As we plant the Word of God in our minds, it will take root and we will find ourselves saying what God says."

> "If you abide in My word, you are My disciples indeed. And you shall know the truth, and the truth shall make you free" (John 8:31,32).

In spite of the fact that believers at times may act according to the pattern of the old self, if they are truly born again and "in Christ," they are new persons in relationship to God and in relationship to themselves. A change of heart is the beginning. Our flaws, character dark spots and inside problems need to be exposed to the power of the Holy Spirit and the work of the cross of Christ in our lives. Sin and character flaws can spin around in our emotional worlds, disrupting our lives, ruining our relationships and causing us to avoid our destinies. They grow and spread like a disease. When these inside things spin out of control, life becomes unmanageable and the pattern we find inside becomes very noticeable to everyone else outside.

When Leonardo da Vinci was working on The Last Supper, he asked a young man named Pietri Bandinelli, who was a chorister in the Milan Cathedral, to sit for the character of Christ. Da Vinci spent the next 25 years working on the painting. He finally had only one character left to paint—Judas Iscariot. After searching and searching for the right person to sit for the character of Judas, the great artist noticed a man in the streets of Rome who he asked to be his model. His shoulders were bent toward the ground. He had a cold, hard, evil look on his face. He looked just like da Vinci's conception of Judas.

When the man was brought into Leonardo da Vinci's studio, he began to look around as if he were recalling incidents of years gone by. Finally, he turned and with a look of sad discover said, "Maestro, I was in this studio 25 years ago. I then sat for Christ.[4]

Many people claim to be Christians just because they are "in church," but real change cannot happen until we are "in Christ." Only when we are "in Christ" can we be all that we are intended for "in church."

Language describes a person whose life is out of control with the word "dysfunctional." We call alcoholism "a disease." We call people with unmanageable life problems "dysfunctional individuals," believing that, because of the root problems in their lives, they need many years and maybe even a lifetime of counseling or some other kind of support system to carry them through life. I would like to protest that belief by agreeing with God's Word which says that if a dysfunctional person is "in Christ," he or she has a new root and a chance to become a brand new person.

Do you know the story of anyone who tried to change but could not change permanently until he or she got saved?? The Lamb's Book of Life contains a library full of these stories.

Inside Thoughts

Change in your inside world generates a transformation that will affect the outside motion. The thoughts in my head, the thoughts I struggle with are the first thoughts that I must recognize and put away. Some of the thoughts that you must dash down to the ground and stomp on, maybe as follows:

+ I don't know what my problems are.

+ I don't care what my problems are and I don't care to change.

+ I can't see what my problems are so how can I change them?

+ I don't accept anyone's opinion about my character, my flaws or my destructive attitudes. People should just mind their own business.

+ This is too hard for me. I don't want to work on this right now.

+ This flaw won't make any difference. I can't change anyway, so quit talking with me about it.

+ I wish the Bible were true for me. I wish I could believe what it says about me. But I can't, so don't tell me what it says.

+ I can't seem to receive grace and mercy. I feel guilt all of the time, shame most of the time and condemnation a lot of the time.

+ I've tried so many times but the weaknesses in my life keep popping up. I am weary of these weaknesses so I think I'll just accept them and live as a weak person.

These are destructive and devilish thoughts that can flood the minds of people who have no control over their inner worlds. Remember: inside cleansing requires inside work! Inside change requires an inside Christ. If you are "in Christ," you are "in change"— you are in transformation and you must put faith in what God has said in His written Word about changing your inside life.

THE INSIDE PROBLEM: THE SIN NATURE

The Bible is clear as to our core problem: the sin nature that has infected every person. The inside problem is not due to a personality defect, or your environment, or even your family tree. It's because of sin, and it's real. The inside problem as Scripture sees it:

For the flesh lusts against the Spirit, and the Spirit against the flesh; and these are contrary to one another, so that you do not do the things that you wish (Gal. 5:17).

The flesh may be defined as existence apart from God, a life dominated by sin or a drive opposed to God. The flesh is self-reliant rather than God-dependent. It is self-centered rather than God-centered.

As Jeremiah 17:9 says, "The heart is deceitful above all things, and desperately wicked; who can know it?" Humankind is depraved. Every aspect of yours and my being was corrupted and we can do nothing to save ourselves. We can't change our wicked hearts. The inside problem of every person is a sin problem. Our hearts can only change through Christ. We must believe that as we accept Christ and begin to live in Him, the inside work is already begun:

> Colossians 2:6,7: As you have therefore received Christ Jesus the Lord, so walk in Him, rooted and built up in Him and established in the faith, as you have been taught, abounding in it with thanksgiving.
>
> Ezekiel 36:26: I will give you a new heart and put a new spirit within you; I will take the heart of stone out of your flesh and give you a heart of flesh.

When we begin to live "in Christ," our lives are regenerated. I will explain it like this: Outside of Christ, we are like a car that tries to push itself according to self will. But when we are in Christ, He empowers us so that where we once had no power over sin, we now have the power to chose to obey God. Regeneration of the person who is spiritually dead must originate with God, who is life. Change is sure, change is steady and ultimately the changing work of God will win out over our inner messed up worlds if we allow it.

The word "regeneration" means change. Regeneration is a change wrought in us by God, not an autonomous act performed by us for ourselves. Repentance plus faith plus the Holy Spirit work equals regeneration. We're not talking about a self-help method found in the hundreds and possibly thousands of self-help, change-yourself books that are on the market. Real change is an inner-heart change that happens through the real work of the Holy Spirit as we yield to Him.

INSIDE WORK IS ALREADY BEGUN

When you are in Christ, you are a new person with a new relationship to God. You are new in yourself. You can change. You don't need to accept any of your past habits as unchangeable. Don't say, "I'll just learn to live with them." No! A thousand times no. Never learn to live with these flaws, these destructive habits. They are not your inheritance. God does not want you to learn to live with them. He wants you to learn to destroy them by the power of the Holy Spirit.

The new you is already planted like a seed in the ground. Ultimately, that tree will be exactly where the planted seed has grown to be a mighty tree. The seed of Christ has been planted in you and you will become a mighty oak, a mighty tree, bearing much fruit for Christ. You have a new Master who will prune you until you branch out in righteousness.

As believers, we have actually changed the propensities of our deepest desires. They are now oriented toward God instead of self and sin. Your flesh lies to you and tries to manipulate you into believing your sinful impulses. Do not obey your impulses but believe in the work of God. God will not quit working on you. According to Philippians 1:6, you can be "confident of this very thing, that He who has begun a good work in you will complete it until the day of Jesus Christ."

Inside Change Requires Faith Action

J. I. Packer said, "It is a part of healthy Christian experience to enjoy a continually increasing degree of deliverance from sins! Few things afford the Christian such relief and encouragement as the memory of sins that once ruled him, but which he has conquered by the power of the Spirit of God."

Inside cleansing is not attained by religious acts. This is what the Bible has to say:

Colossians 3:10: And have put on the new man who is renewed in knowledge according to the image of Him who created him.

Romans 6:14: For sin shall not have dominion over you, for you are not under law but under grace.

1 John 4:4: You are of God, little children, and have overcome them, because He who is in you is greater than he who is in the world.

Inside cleansing is not attained by religious perfectionism. It is not attained by the ways of the Matthew 23 Pharisees who dealt only with the externals of religion and the outside of the cup. True cleansing is attained by the power of Christ and the grace of God that is put into us through repentance and accepting the Bible as true. Cleansing comes when we fall so deeply in love with Jesus that we don't want to hold anything back.

While visiting in Haiti, Dale A. Hayes heard a Haitian pastor illustrate to his congregation the need for total commitment to Christ. He told of a certain man who wanted to sell his house for $2,000. Another man badly wanted it, but couldn't afford the full price. After much haggling, the owner agreed to sell the house for half the asking price with just one stipulation: he would retain ownership of one small nail protruding from just over the door.

After several years, the original owner wanted the house back, but the new owner was unwilling to sell. So the first owner went out, found the carcass of a dead dog, and hung it from the single nail he still owned. Soon the house became uninhabitable, and the family was forced to sell the house to the owner of the nail.

The Haitian pastor's conclusion: "If we leave the devil with even one small peg in our lives, he will return to hang his rotting garbage on it, making it unfit for Christ's habitation."

The closer we come to Jesus, the more He will expose the dead dogs and unholy pegs so that we will repent and apply the Word of God for change. As someone has said, "He loves us just as we are but He loves us too much too leave us there." He changes us from the inside out as we focus more and more on the one who lives inside of us.

The scribes and Pharisees were the religious perfectionists of their day. They focused on the outside—rules rather than relationship. They had external behavior down to a science, but their hearts were like the insides of a tomb, reeking of dead dogs.

You don't change by focusing on outward behavior, you change by focusing on His nature. Only after He changes who you are and makes you a partaker of His divine nature will you be able to change your behavior.

Let's look at Matthew 23:26-28 again:

"Blind Pharisee, first cleanse the inside of the cup and dish, that the outside of them may be clean also. Woe to you, scribes and Pharisees, hypocrites! For you are like whitewashed tombs which indeed appear beautiful outwardly, but inside are full of dead men's bones and all uncleanness. Even so you also outwardly appear righteous to men, but inside you are full of hypocrisy and lawlessness."

Jesus is saying, outwardly you look attractive, appear fair to the eye, and look fine. People think you are good. You have the right look. But there is something wrong that people can't see. Within is all rottenness, every kind of decay and foulness. On the inside you are full of every wicked thing. You have become excellent in hiding that which really exists inside, but sooner or later you will slip and something will happen and that which is on the inside will appear in your behavior and people will understand that there is foulness and every kind of decay resting in the character of that person.

We all need to be blatantly honest with ourselves and with God, asking for the grace of the Holy Spirit to change our Phariseelike natures and to change us from being hypocrites into being transparent believers who are honest to God and authentic with others.

Our whole society is built upon appearances: physical looks, financial status, houses, cars, clothes. It's all about perception. Our society is poised for a Matthew 23 look, an outward look, an external look. Jesus is trying to establish a Law of First Things, a law of single focus. We need to be first and foremost interested with our inner selves, the hidden part that only God sees. This is the Law of First Things. Learn it and your life will be blessed. You will become the kind of disciple that Christ can trust and that people can follow. Reverse this law and you will be a Pharisee in the making, calling attention to the external or the visible. Ultimately, you will lead people astray and your life will not count for the Kingdom of God.

> *"We need to be first and foremost interested with our inner selves, the hidden part that only God sees."*

FIVE INSIDE DESTRUCTIVE SIN HABITS

Jesus exposes five habits that the Pharisees would not deal with. There are many more sinful habits but these could be root problems:

1. Extortion: Living to please oneself

The Greek word for extortion is the word *"harpag"* (har-pag-éy), which can mean pillage, extortion, spoiling. The verb form means to seize or to take by force, plunder, rob, or seize something that does not belong to you. The root word has the idea that you are seizing it for yourself, for your own greed, not even out of need, but just out of lustful desire. Luke 11:39 says, "But the Lord said to him, 'Now you Pharisees make the outside of the cup and dish clean, but your inward part is full of greed and wickedness.'"

2. Self-indulgence: Living without self-control

The Greek word Jesus mentions immediately after extortion is *akrasia*, which means a lack of self-restraint and self-control, living a life in excess. The opposite is the word *"egkrates"* (eng-krat-áce), which combines two words, *"en"* (in or through) with *"kratos"* (power, usually God's). The meaning of *enkrates* is to be under self-control through God's power. Thus, lack of self-control could be seen as lack of walking in the power of God that enables you to act with restraint. We also know that self-control is a fruit of the spirit (see Gal. 5:23), something that has grown from a seed and is nurtured by the life and the spirit within the person.

3. Uncleanness: Living an impure life

Uncleanness is translated from the Greek word *"akatharsia,"* which is impurity, either physically or morally. It is an uncleanness. The opposite of impurity is *katharos.* In ancient literature it was used to speak of tenants keeping their houses in good condition.

Here Jesus is referring to a person who is destroying his or her house. I am sure you have been to a house where the yard is unkept and the house is unpainted. Inside, the rooms are disastersous because the house has been taken advantage of and has fallen apart. Sometimes this happens when a person is just renting a house and has no ownership, no investment in it.

This is what we reveal in our attitudes when we don't take ownership of what God is doing in us. We just treat the work of God as if we are a renter, a tenant. We are to be very careful not to destroy the house that God is building:

> Romans 6:19: I speak in human terms because of the weakness of your flesh. For just as you presented your members as slaves of uncleanness, and of lawlessness leading to more lawlessness, so now present your members as slaves of righteousness for holiness.
> Ephesians 4:19: Who, being past feeling, have given themselves over to lewdness, to work all uncleanness with greediness.

4. Hypocrisy: Living a life of deceit

The Greek word for hypocrisy in Matthew 23:28 is *"hupokrisis,"* which is a person acting under a feigned part or living in deceit. It can be used to speak of a pretender, or of an actor in a staged play. In religion,

it denotes someone who acts the part of someone that he or she neither is nor that he or she may be or perhaps nor what he or she would
desire to be. Jesus refers to these kinds of people as hypocrites and
whitened sepulchers.

As Jesus was giving this teaching, the Passover was just around the
corner. That meant that the pilgrims streaming into Jerusalem from
every direction saw many whitewashed tombs covered with powered
lime dust. A few weeks earlier the burial places had been made to look
spic and span, neat and trim. They had been conspicuously dusted with
the white lime lest any pilgrim should render himself ceremoniously
unclean by inadvertently coming into contact with a corpse or human
bone (see Num. 19:16; Luke 11:44). Yet on the inside of such graves the
flesh of corpses decomposed until all that was left was bones.

Jesus says this is what hypocrites looks like. Outwardly they seem
to be righteous, but inwardly they are filled with lawlessness. What
really counts as it says in 1 Samuel 16:7, is what a person is on the
inside, morally and spiritually. God looks on the heart, but man looks
on the outward. The words "whitened sepulchers" refers to living
behind a facade, appearing to be one thing on the outside but actually
being a different thing within. While whitened sepulchers is a very sim-
ilar concept to hypocrisy, the whitened sepulcher emphasizes covering
up the death and impurity inside. It is living with the outside changed,
but not the inside.

Jesus tells the Pharisees, "For you are like," meaning you exactly
resemble a whitened sepulcher. The parallel is complete. Jesus has
again riveted His teaching in a sure place. There is no moving around
it. You must face it. If you were a hypocrite, you understood what Jesus
meant and you were able to judge your life—that is, if you were willing
to judge your life. Jesus always addressed hypocrisy:

> Matthew 23:28: "Even so you also outwardly appear righteous
> to men, but inside you are full of hypocrisy and lawless-
> ness."
>
> Mark 12:15: "Shall we pay, or shall we not pay?" But He, know-
> ing their hypocrisy, said to them, "Why do you test Me?
> Bring Me a denarius that I may see it."

Luke 12:1: In the meantime, when an innumerable multitude of people had gathered together, so that they trampled one another, He began to say to His disciples first of all, "Beware of the leaven of the Pharisees, which is hypocrisy."

(See also Gal. 2:13; 1 Tim. 4:2; 1 Pet. 2:1).

5. Lawlessness: Living in violation of God's laws

The Greek word "*anomia*" means simply a violation of law or wickedness. It is also translated iniquity, which is a transgression of the law that Jesus calls unrighteousness and lawlessness. This definition of sin sets forth its essential character as the rejecter of the law, or rejection of the will of God and the substitution of the will of self.

There are two aspects of lawless living. The first is outwardly "righteous" acts that are an inward violation of the law of God. As Jesus reminds us in Matthew 7:23–"And then I will declare to them, 'I never knew you; depart from Me, you who practice lawlessness!'"–and Matthew 13:41–"The Son of Man will send out His angels, and they will gather out of His kingdom all things that offend, and those who practice lawlessness"–God sees our inward lawlessness.

The other aspect of lawless living is outwardly "righteous" acts without an inward love for God. Matthew 24:12 says, "And because lawlessness will abound, the love of many will grow cold." Jesus says in the Scripture that the lawlessness or the violation of God's law can become a way of inward life–that is, there is no love for the law of God in the heart. There is no bending of the character with regard to those laws in the hidden areas of life. There is only an outward observance of the laws to make people think that you really do love the law of God, when in fact the laws have no influence over your life.

First John 3:4 says that "Whoever commits sin also commits lawlessness, and sin is lawlessness." Let's turn to God for a continual change of inner person. If the Holy Spirit has allowed you to see areas that need immediate attention, begin to respond to God now. Live according to the flesh or live according to the Spirit. You chose. You must live in Christ or out of Christ.

Destructive habit patterns, double-mindedness, unstable emotions, impurity, outbursts of anger, stubbornness, pride, rebellion, strife, and any other work of the flesh can be brought under the work of the Cross. But first we must cleanse the inside, the hidden, the real, the roots. The inside will influence every other area of our lives. First cleanse the inside and then the outside will be clean also. Listen to the words of King David in Psalm 51:6:

You desire truth in the inward parts, and in the hidden part
You will make me to know wisdom.

God wants you to know Him authentically in the inward parts because that is where He knows you. Jesus, when teaching the beatitudes, confirmed this principle with Matthew 5:8:

"Blessed are the pure in heart for they shall see God."

Other translations say:

J. B. Phillips: "Happy are the utterly sincere for they will see God."

Young's: "Happy are the clean in heart because they shall see God."

Barkley: "Blessed are those whose motives are absolutely unmixed, whose minds are utterly sincere, who are completely and totally single-minded."

Our goal as true believers is to be pure in heart, not just appearing to be pure, but coming closer to an inward purity. We are to be increasingly free from mixture or anything that soils or corrupts our motives or desires. We are to be progressively more free from any false or insincere thing that would blemish our character. Jesus wants us to develop (it is a process!) a singleness of heart. He wants us to pursue an honesty which has no hidden motive, no selfish interests. He wants us to become more and more authentic, to become true and open in all things so that we are real and genuine as opposed to unreal and fake.

The inside first, we must first return to the ground of faith, return to the Cross, return to the simplicity of forgiveness, return to the power of His blood, return to total trust in Him. Then, we will have a pure conscience, a pure mind, a pure spirit. And that which is inside of us will become so clean that it pours out a fresh, sparkling, clear, spiritual water so that all who drink of this river will be refreshed and encouraged.

Christianity is seen by many to be weak and ineffective, both in our own nation of America as well as in many nations of the world. The world has yet to see true Christianity expressed as Jesus intended it to be expressed. Even in the Early Church? Yes, even in the Early Church. When it does, it will impact our society in an unprecedented way. However this begins from the heart, not from programs or church buildings or from the traditional religious activities in which we have engaged ourselves. God works from the inside out.

The righteousness that God requires begins inside with a change of heart. God is certainly interested first of all with the heart, more than just the action, but the action will follow the heart change when the heart has truly been changed (see 1 Chron. 28:9; 2 Chron. 16:9; Prov. 16:2; 1 Cor. 4:4; 1 Cor. 4:5).

If the inside is wrong then the outside doesn't matter. Jesus' position is revolutionary. He did not set in motion a social political revolution, but one emerging from the heart, from a radical change in a man's thinking resulting from conversion and sanctification.

Notes

1 Robert J. Morgan, ed., *Nelson's Complete Book of Stories, Illustrations & Quotes* (Nashville: Thomas Nelson, 2000), p. 72.

2 Marilyn Abrahamm, *First We Quit Our Jobs* (New York: Dell Publishing, 1997).

3 E. Stanley Jones, *In Christ* http://www.posword.org/articles/others/inchrsj1.shtml

4 Jim Burns and Greg McKinnon, *Illustrations, Stories and Quotes* (Ventura, Calif.: Gospel Light, 1997), p. 81.

First Day of the Week
Aligning with His Body

Then, the same day at evening, being the first day of the week,
when the doors were shut where the disciples were assembled, for fear of the Jews,
Jesus came and stood in the midst, and said to them, "Peace be with you."
—John 20:19

Someone once said, "Our great-grandparents called it the holy Sabbath. Our grandparents called it the Lord's Day. Our parents called it Sunday. And we call it the weekend."[1]

> In the early days of the Nazi domination of Europe, the British Parliament still considered weekends their own. Britian's ruling class left London for their country estates and didn't want to be bothered. It created no small problem, for crucial decisions could not be made in crisis because those in authority were unavailable. Winston Churchill, frustrated beyond words, complained, "that Britian's rulers continued to take its weekends in the country, while Hitler takes his countries in the weekends."
>
> When we neglect God's business on Sundays to pursue our own leisure, it gives Satan a free hand.[2]

The "first day" principle shows the importance of placing God first in our week. Without it we are prone to be "weak" for another week.

Giving Him the first day is symbolic of allowing Him to take first place in the other six days, because the first day sets the rest of the week in order. The first day is a day for honoring God as Lord, a day for remembering our covenant with Christ, a day of renewal and rededication. To respect the Lord's day is to respect the gathering of God's people.

Obviously, this assemblage could take place on a day other than Sunday, but Sunday has become the symbolic day, not just today but all the way back to the beginnings of the New Testament.

We do not worship the day itself because the New Testament teaches us that God can be worshiped any day of the seven and should be respected all seven days of the week. Nevertheless, a day is to be set aside for the gathering of God's people. From the book of Acts until present, that day has been Sunday. For some it is different, but for most of Christianity, Sunday has been a respected day of worship for more than 2000 years.

John 20:19 says, "Then, the same day at evening, being the first day of the week, when the doors were shut where the disciples were assembled, for fear of the Jews, Jesus came and stood in the midst, and said to them, 'Peace be with you.'" As we see here the disciples were gathered together and Jesus appeared to the group.

In Acts 20:7 we read, "Now on the first day of the week, when the disciples came together to break bread, Paul, ready to depart the next day, spoke to them and continued his message until midnight." The Early Church gathered on the first day of the week to break bread, to worship and pray and to be taught the Word of God. First Corinthians 16:2 provides another example of the church honoring the first day of the week:

On the first day of the week let each one of you lay something aside, storing up as he may prosper, that there be no collections when I come.

Though many of the first Christians continued their worship in synagogues on the Sabbath, most of the Early Church met on the first day with consistency and commitment. The first day became the new day for the new covenant group, a day of rejoicing, breaking of bread, singing, praying, receiving teaching and doctrine and fellowshipping one with another. In the book of Acts and the Epistles, the first day was considered a special, sacred day, as it should be to all twenty-first-century Christians.

Barna Research Group made the following observation of our nation:

> In 1986, 42 percent of adults attended a church service during a typical week in January. Attendance rose steadily, reaching a peak of 49 percent in 1991, before beginning a very slow but steady descent back to 40 percent in January, 2000.[3]

And in the May 25, 1994 edition of *USA Today*, we found this statistic concerning church-going in America: "48 percent of church goers attend an average of only once a month." Why would people be committed to working 20 days a month, or committed to going to school 20 days a month, and yet be committed to going to church only one day or half a day of the month?

For every person raised without religion who adopts a church, statistics say that three people forsake the church for no institutional affiliation. Why are so many Christians forsaking the assembling together with fellow Christians on a consistent weekly basis? Members of Willowcreek Community Church in Willowcreek, Illinois, which is pastored by Bill Hybels, did a door-to-door survey around their church to ask the question, If you don't go to church, why? The five biggest reasons given by people surveyed were:

1. It's boring
2. It's irrelevant
3. The church asks for money all the time
4. I'm too busy already
5. I feel awkward at church

These responses can be true on some level for many millions of people in our nation and maybe in other nations of the world. The church must have a spiritual level of relevancy, impact and truth that changes people's lives and challenges them in ways that impact their lives. We can change the perception that the church is boring and irrelevant.

A shift has occurred in the mind-set of people about what they want out of church. Most people want to know more about what they can get out of church, than what they can give. Church has become one more consumer commodity. Often, Church services cease to be a place for us to serve God and our neighbors, and instead become a place where people expect to purchase the best: inspiring worship, good music, moving sermons, quality childcare (as if we buy God and not vice versa).

The church *should* have inspiring worship, great music, moving sermons and quality childcare. These things are part of the excellence of the church. But when the church uses these things only to encourage attendance and not as a New Testament commitment for serving and sacrificing in order to lift other members of the Body, the church becomes a consumer commodity.

We want to develop in the church a Psalms 27:4-6 attitude:

One thing I have desired of the LORD, that will I seek: that I may dwell in the house of the LORD all the days of my life, to behold the beauty of the LORD, and to inquire in His temple. For in the time of trouble he shall hide me in His pavilion; in the secret place of His tabernacle he shall hide me; he shall set me high upon a rock. And now my head shall be lifted up above my enemies all around me; therefore I will offer sacrifices of joy in His tabernacle; I will sing, yes, I will sing praises to the LORD.

The goal and vision of every church should be to develop Christians who have a "one thing" desire toward the Lord and toward His house, Christians who run to the Lord and to the church in times of trouble, and Christians who will learn to bring the sacrifices of joy and the sacrifices of praise into the House of God as part of their commitment to the first day. (See also Psalm 84:1,2,4,10).

The Bible says that "Those who are planted in the house of the LORD shall flourish in the courts of our God" (Ps. 92:13). Are you planted in the House of the Lord and flourishing in the courts of God? Are you developing a first day desire?

First Day Commitment Thieves

John 10:10 says, "The thief does not come except to steal, and to kill, and to destroy. I have come that they may have life, and that they may have it more abundantly." So let's look at some of the thieves that are keeping us from a first day commitment.

Hurried Lifestyle

One of the first things to be cast aside from a hurried lifestyle is a commitment to the Lord's Day. We pray for people to get jobs and to have the provision of God upon their lives, but often the fulfillment of these blessings takes them away from serving and from the kingdom of God. Instead of using their jobs for God's purposes, they allow their jobs to use them. When these people become successful, they have difficulty finding the time to serve in Bible studies or small group leadership or worship or choirs or bands or childcare or evangelism or feeding the hungry—areas to bless people don't fit into their normal hurried lifestyles. They just can't fit it in. Usually, the more successful people become, the busier their lives become, and the less time they give to the House of God.

> "We pray for people to get jobs and to have the provision of God upon their lives, but often the fulfillment of these blessings takes them away from serving and from the kingdom of God."

We need to address our time commitments and our apathy toward the church. We need to address seriously why we don't develop our spiritual gifts in order to extend the kingdom of God and serve in the House of God. We need to address the issues of apathy toward the Lord's Day and our inconsistency in gathering with God's people.

Entertainment Lifestyle

Creative lifestyles have brought time pressures in such a multitude of activities that its almost mind-boggling. Statistics say that in most homes an average of nine hours a day is spent with media, television, radio, CDs, tapes and computers. Nine hours a day! One hour per day average is spent on-line alone. People are now working from 47-55 hours a week, different from 15 years ago when the average was 38-40 hours a week. Many people are spending at least 70 minutes a day in their cars driving to sport activities, shopping, work or social events.

Our culture is changing so fast that many people complain that they feel like they turned around and missed the last 10 years.

Breaking the Hurried Habit

Set at least one day aside per week to honor the Lord, meditate, pause, take a break, listen to the voice of your conscience. Rest in the Lord. Allow the Holy Spirit to tune in and do some remodeling work on the interior of your soul. If you have no down time to work on the interior part of the your life, the exterior will take control and the internal will wither up. One reason visiting the House of the Lord is so important is that it helps us to step out of the busyness of our routines and into the peace of God's sanctuary. As we see in the Early Church of Acts 2, it is also a day for serving others and being evangelistic in our faith.

We come to the house of God to enjoy His presence, to hear His word, to meditate on His word, to pray and to sing and worship, to allow the Holy Spirit to speak to us through the gifts of the Spirit and through the preaching of the Word. Our souls are renewed, our spirits are strengthened. We see people who need us as much as we need them to give and to receive encouragement. We also have the privilege of giving our finances through our tithes and offerings, recognizing that God has trusted us to be stewards of what we have.

Weekly church attendance reminds us that we are stewards, life managers of what God has given us. We don't own our lives, nor do we own our possessions. God is the owner of all things and we are His servants. If you and I are reminded of these and other principles once a week, instead of one time every two months, we will be more apt to live out God's precepts and walk in Kingdom alignment.

For example, the following testimony illustrates how a man even found his way back to sobriety through weekly church attendance:

I was saved on July 25, 1999 at Promise Keepers. The Lord then led me to City Bible Church where my life changed completely. Thank you, Lord.

I've been a member of City Bible Church since December 12, 1999; I came just as I was—an alcoholic of 7 years. I was attending church and an awesome cell group weekly. Nonetheless, regardless of my faithfulness to church-related activities, I was even more faithful to the alcohol. The following Spring, I sensed the Lord wanting to use me in some way but my drinking was in the way, I prayed about my addiction, believing that I needed AA or another support group to assist me in what I thought would be a daily battle.

But the Lord spoke to me, saying, "Confess your addiction to your cell group and you will be set free." I was so afraid of being rejected. Throughout the following six months, Pastor Frank's sermons seemed to be directly aimed at me; they were like weekly counseling sessions. Regrettably, I was still a full-blown alcoholic, daily increasing my consumption. Of course the enemy knew that the church and my cell group were being used to uphold me for my day of deliverance.

In the Fall of 2000, our cell group planned a weekend retreat and because the cell group consisted mostly of non-smokers, my wife and I thought the occasion would be a good time to attempt to quit smoking and to TRY to quit drinking. As the retreat drew near, I sensed the Lord telling me again and again, "Confess your addiction to your cell group and you will be set free." Though I felt quite comfortable with the cell group members, I was still afraid to confess that I was an alcoholic. My wife, bless her heart, had already shared with some trusted cell members about my addiction and they were praying for me.

Fortunately, my wife never demanded that I quit but she had voiced her concern several times to me. My wife stood by me daily and she was about to be rewarded for her steadfastness as much as I was. On October 13th, we left for the Coast and a weekend of fellowship. That whole weekend the spirit was moving as relationships were strengthened. On the last day, during our final time of prayer, the cell leader asked for specific prayer requests– that's when the spirit moved on me. I began to cry as my confession rolled off my lips and onto the hearts of the cell group members. The next 10 minutes of prayer were so anointed and the presence of God was so obvious that it would have been impossible not to be delivered.

I was delivered from alcohol that day and my wife and I were both delivered from cigarettes. The relationships formed in the church and in the cell group were a pivotal source of strength for my deliverance. I thank God for City Bible Church, for Pastor Frank and for the cell group members who loved me even when I felt that I was not worthy of their love.

My own journey into church as a Jesus freak is another good example of why we need to attend church. I accepted the Lord out in Riverside, California at major-league baseball player Albie Pearson's home, during the Jesus Movement. Later, a group of us met for Bible studies at Albie's home. Eventually, we started having Friday-night meetings and saw many, many young people getting saved. The problem began when people were confronted with the importance of applying biblical principles. As a generation unto ourselves, we didn't know how to disciple each other. What we needed was the local church. We needed the experience of older believers to become a safeguard, a protection for us. Regrettably, because we didn't understand the importance of church, we lost most of the harvest. However!! I can tell you of one who went into the church and trained for ministry–me. This little Jesus freak went on to become a church planter and a church builder. Why? Because I saw that only those who went on and became involved in churches made it through. Thank God for the local church–it instilled in me the values I embrace today.

Changing Values

The values of the twenty-first century are changing. By "value," I mean something that is esteemed and thought to be of worth. A change in values has caused a change in lifestyles. Three trends have become apparent concerning this first thing called church attendance:

1. Irregular attendance among the regulars
2. Multiple church attendance (people attending 2, 3, 4 or even 5 churches irregularly as they "church shop" to get the best from each)
3. Nonchurch spiritual activities that replace church commitment

People turn on the television church, or phone a friend or two and call that "church." According to the New Testament, this does not qualify as "church."

We have had a change of values from traditional values to new values. Traditional values of absolutes that govern right and wrong have been exchanged for new values in which relativism governs morality.

TRADITIONAL	NEW
– Absolutes govern right and wrong	– Relativism governs morality
– Committed relationships	– Relationships of convenience
– Trust based on reputation	– Self-protection and suspicion
– Loyalty without personal gain	– Loyalty to one's self first
– Money related to true worth	– Time on self is now true worth
– Benefit community over self	– Self first, community second
– Your word is your bond	– Your word shifts with circumstances
– Investment in the long term	– Investment in the short term
– Wisdom of ages valued	– Tradition dismissed
– God the center of all matters	– Humanity the center of reality
– The church is worthy of my life	– My life is given to many causes. Perhaps church will be one.

As a result of coming face to face with evil, some people are beginning to reject the platitudes of relativism. They are seeking a more spiritual and Christian center, but they are also confused about what is personally important, what is culturally significant and what is morally non-negotiable. Even within the church, most people are confused about Kingdom values and Kingdom priorities and how they should set these values into their lives.

Moreover, our society is struggling not only with the consequences of a values shift, but also with the core issues that make it unsettling to address the question of changed values. The Boomers energetically created and integrated alternative philosophies and perspectives into their own lives. Even as America was waging the bullet-less battles of the cold war with the Soviet empire, the Boomers were simultaneously battling a values war, a revolution of the heart among the people of the nation. I believe that the tragedy of September 11th has galvanized a wake up call. It's time to rethink our values.

Loving God and loving God's people is a value. Loving church and setting aside a day to worship is a value. Being consistent and faithful to that commitment is a value. You esteem it to be worthy of your life. It is a law, a principle you will not break. You highly esteem this first day principle, thus you set other things aside to make sure that you and your spouse and your family, find themselves in the House of God weekly, all the days of your life. This is a value.

THE SPIRIT OF THE TWENTY-FIRST CENTURY

The spirit of the twenty-first century is working against the Holy Spirit. It is working against your commitment to the first day of the week, your commitment to honor God, to receive teaching, to give worship and to fellowship with God's people. Who do you think is working against you all the time to keep you out of the House of God? It certainly isn't God or the Holy Spirit. It is the spirit of the twenty-first century. It is the spirit that finds its root in hell itself.

The Spirit of Humanism

Humanism is the "religion" of the social, educational and political elite, by and large.

Let me quote from the *Humanist Manifesto*:

> We consider the religious forms and ideas of our fathers no longer adequate. The quest for the good life is still the central task for mankind. Man is at least becoming aware that he alone is responsible for the realization of the world of his dreams, that he has within himself the power for its achievement. He must set intelligence and will to the task.[4]

The *Humanist Manifesto* is a manifesto against the Word of God and God Himself, written by humanists who esteem themselves higher than God. All these problems blend into a philosophy that can be summed up in the statement: I don't need God. Humanists believe prayer to God is unproved, outmoded faith. Salvation is harmful, diverting people with false hope.

Obviously, this root in our society will not respect God, the church or the Bible. And so we see this disrespect blossoming in our society today. In our schools, prayer has been banned and reading the Bible has been forbidden. We are a multi-religious country instead of a Christian country. The humanist spirit works against the Holy Spirit. The spirit of humanism is first of all a hellish-spirit that establishes itself in people's lives as a spirit of self-centeredness instead of God-and-others centeredness with the desire to please, serve and live for oneself. This problem of self-interest is the very spirit of hell itself rising up to get what hell wants—the possession of the human soul and the human life.

The spirit of humanism is the spirit of independence and freedom from any restraints. It is the desire to be one's own master without any accountability to anyone, to answer

> *"The spirit of humanism is the spirit of independence and freedom from any restraints. It is the desire to be one's own master without any accountability to anyone, to answer only to self."*

only to self. Satan's goal was to usurp God's authority and to rule all of creation, including humanity.

The spirit of humanism is the spirit of solitariness. It is the desire to live for oneself, to isolate one's actions and energies from the community of God, as Satan did. Problems such as isolated, apathetic individuals and fragmented families often result. Families and individuals relocate frequently, detaching themselves out of restlessness and causing a lack of roots. This mobility brings a sense of detachment from their neighborhoods, cities, churches, extended families—everyone but their own private existences. This same restlessness is seen in church hopping where people change church families without biblical mandate or Holy Spirit guidance.

The Spirit of Alienation

People can be saved, but alienated and withdrawn from the church. People can be saved, but maintain an independent attitude and lifestyle. Even though they have come into a salvation experience, they have not changed their lifestyles from that of the corrupted culture to the kingdom of God lifestyle. People can be saved, but not mature in church growth, not maturing with the Body of Christ in serving one another, fellowshipping, sacrificing and being rooted and grounded in the church. People can be saved, but remain under the former spirit, the spirit of alienation, the spirit of selfishness, the spirit of the devil himself.

The Spirit of the Kingdom of God

The spirit of our age may be kicking against the kingdom of God and against the church, but Jesus said, "On this rock I will build My church, and the gates of Hades shall not prevail against it" (Matt. 16:18). As the spirit of this age kicks against the Kingdom and against the church, many people see the church in great peril from a variety of dangers: secularism, politics, heresies and just plain old sin. They forget that the church is built upon a rock over which the gates of hell itself shall never prevail.

As a believer, you should recognize the working of the spirit of our culture in your life. Be renewed in your mind so that you can war against the false philosophies that are trying to shake your life. In Ephesians 2:2 Paul says, "In which you once walked according to the course of this world, according to the prince and the power of the air, the spirit who now works in the sons of disobedience." We used to walk under the course of this world, under the spirit that works in people living a lifestyle of sin and disobedience, but we are no longer under that spirit. We have been delivered by the power of the Cross. We have been delivered by the Holy Spirit from these dangers that try to shape our lives.

Listen to Romans 12:1,2 from *The Amplified Bible*:

I appeal to you therefore brethren and beg of you in view of all the mercies of God to make a decisive dedication of your bodies presenting all your members and faculties as a living sacrifice, holy, devoted, consecrated and well pleasing to God, which is your reasonable, rational, intelligent service and spiritual worship. You are not to be conformed to this world, this age, fashioned after and adapted to its external, superficial customs. You are to be transformed, that is changed by the entire renewal of your mind, by its new ideal and its new attitude, so that you may prove for yourselves what is the good and acceptable and perfect will of God, and acceptable and perfect in his sight for you.

DECISIONS THAT KEEP THE FIRST DAY A FIRST THING

We need to make some decisions that make and keep the first day a first thing. We need to believe what Jesus has taught us, that this is a viable principle which we should esteem and establish in our daily lifestyles. Justin Martyr, one of the Early Church fathers who lived in the second century made the following statement:

And on the day called Sunday, all who live in cities or in the country gather together in one place, and the memoirs of the apostles or the writings of the prophets are read... But Sunday is the day on which we all hold a common assembly, because it is the first day of the week on which God...made the world; and Jesus Christ our Savior on the same day rose from the dead.[5]

The Early Church, that is the church in the book of Acts and the church of the second century that Justin Martyr and other Early Church fathers were part of, esteemed Sunday as the Lord's day and set this day aside for worship and reading of the God's Word.

In the twenty-first century, we have church services on Saturday night, Sunday morning, Sunday nights, Wednesday nights, Thursday nights, Friday nights. We have churches that hold regular church services weekly on just about any day of the week. I'm not trying to establish Sunday as the only time to worship, I am trying to establish a principle to set one time aside per week to worship with the Body of Christ. For you, that might be a Friday night service, or a Saturday night service, or a Sunday morning service. It is not the day itself, as much as the principle to commit yourself to a weekly gathering with the people of God.

Decide, make a commitment, a consecration.

Decide that you have been placed into one congregation, one body, as a needed member and commit to gathering with that group of people on a weekly basis.

> 1 Corinthians 12:12: For as the body is one and has many members, but all the members of that one body, being many, are one body, so also is Christ.
>
> 1 Corinthians 12:18: But now God has set the members, each one of them, in the body just as He pleased. (*The Amplified Bible* reads, "God has carefully placed each part of the body right where he wanted it.")

Your Importance in the Body of Christ

You are part of the body. The Lord has carefully placed you in the church where you are now worship and fellowship. As an integral part of that body, begin to function with its members, serving, honoring one another, fellowshipping, receiving from and giving to each member of that body. It doesn't matter if it is a small church of 20 or a large church of thousands, you can be involved with the members of that body. Most churches today have small groups of 10 or 15 people that you can commit to and grow with. Even though you might worship with 5,000, 2,000, 1,000 or 500, you can still be involved with a small group of people and also worship with a large group of people. Scripture places an emphasis on staying connected with other believers:

Romans 14:7: For none of us lives to himself, and no one dies to himself.

Ephesians 4:16: From whom the whole body, joined and knit together by what every joint supplies, according to the effective working by which every part does its share, causes growth of the body for the edifying of itself in love.

Someone wrote the following fictitious letter that was to be written to a pastor about a person's attitude towards church and how much that person should attend:

Dear Pastor,

You often stress attendance at worship as being very important for a Christian, but I think a person has a right to miss now and then. I think every person ought to be excused for the following reasons and the number of times indicated:

- Christmas (Sunday before or after) 1
- Independence Day (National holiday) 1
- School opens (One last fling) 1
- Easter (Get away for the holidays) 2
- Mother's Day (Time with my mother) 1
- Father's Day (Time with my father) 1
- School closing (Children need a break) 1
- Family Reunions (Mine and wife's) 3

- Sleep late (Saturday night activities) 4
- Deaths in the family 4
- Anniversary (Second honeymoon) 1
- Sickness (One for each family member) 5
- Business trips (Can't be helped) 4
- Vacation 4
- Children's sports 5
- Bad weather (Too cold, too hot) 4
- Unexpected company (Can't walk out) 5
- Specials on TV (Super Bowl Sunday, etc.) 3

Pastor, that leaves only two Sundays per year. So you can count on us to be in church on the fourth Sunday in February and the third Sunday in August, all things going well.

Sincerely yours,
Faithful Member

Did you get a chuckle out of that letter? Even though it is fictitious, it probably does describe many people's attitudes regarding church attendance. We can all think of many reasons for not making it to church this coming Sunday—even I can and I'm the pastor! If you don't draw the line somewhere and make a commitment or renew your mind to value Sunday, these and other excuses will become strong temptations not to go. You must esteem church attendance worthy of your life and time and commitment and teach your family to do the same. Not only should we attend church on a weekly basis, but we should also have a conviction that we will function in the church that we attend.

Your Function in the Body of Christ

The principle of function again comes out of a value or a conviction. We see ourselves as part of the Body and realize we have a gift and we are important to that church. The local church is an expansion of the Body of Christ, which consists of divinely gifted people. Each one shares the common gift of eternal life and each one has a distinctive gift that enables that person to function in his or her particular God-appointed place. Scripture says:

> 1 Corinthians 12:30: We find God's distribution of gifts is on the same principles of harmony that he has shown in the human body (*J. B. Phillips*).
>
> Romans 12:5,6: So we, numerous as we are, are one body in Christ the Messiah and individually we are parts of one another [mutually dependent on one another]. Having gifts (faculties, talents, qualities) that differ according to the grace given us, let us use them: He whose gift is prophecy, let him prophesy according to the proportion of his faith (*Amp.*).

Decide that you and your family will create a "first day" lifestyle habit and stay with this commitment.

Permit me to quote from the book *Apostolic Constitutions* regarding church life in the second century:

> On the day of the resurrection of the Lord—that is, the Lord's Day—assembly yourself together without fail, giving thanks to God and praising Him for those mercies God has bestowed upon you through Christ.

The first church was a church that decided to create a lifestyle habit that was committed to functioning around the Lord's Day.

In his book *The Body*, Charles Colson, said:

> Membership in a confessing body is fundamental to the faithful Christian life. Failure to do so defies the explicit warning not to forsake "our assembling together." His understanding of this prompted Martin Luther to say, "Apart from the church, salvation is impossible." Not that the church provides salvation; God does. But because the "saved" one can't fulfill what it means to be a Christian apart from the church, membership becomes the

indispensable mark of salvation. "So highly does the Lord esteem the communion of His church," Calvin wrote, "that He considers everyone a traitor and apostate from religion who perversely withdraws himself from any Christian society which preserves the true ministry of the Word and sacraments."[6]

Hebrews 10:25 says, "Not forsaking or neglecting to assemble together as believers, as is the habit of some people, but admonishing–warning, urging and encouraging–one another, and all the more faithfully as you see the day approaching (*Amp.*).

We should not abandon our commitment to the church. We should not neglect our own church attendance because of the cultural enemies that are pressing down upon our life habits. We should not stay away from the church meetings because of fatigue, sickness, headaches, busyness, or simply our addictions to other kinds of pleasure. We need to commit ourselves to the House of God, to the church and become faithful members so that the Church of Jesus Christ can be a bright light in this dark society.

Decide that you will be on time, participate wholeheartedly and be a contributor.

I'm amazed to note how nonchalantly people treat church attendance and when they do attend how casually they treat the clock. People consistently arrive 15, 20 or 30 minutes late. They will come in at the end of worship and sit through the preaching, scurrying out the back door as soon as the last "amen" is said. Some people habitually arrive late every Sunday. What a terrible thing to be teaching our children: it says that the church has no value. And yet, the same people who mosey into church late would never do so at their jobs. If they arrived late three out of five working days, after a few weeks they would find a pink slip sitting on their desks. Of course, the church is not a "hire and fire" institution with regard to its membership. But surely the membership should respect the beginning and the ending times of the church services.

Make a commitment. Commit to being on time. Commit to being involved in the service. Commit to being a wholehearted pray-er and worshiper. Commit to looking to the Lord that He might use you to minister to someone else during church services (see 1 Cor. 14:26; Eph. 4:16).

You are part of the body. Do not be a spectator, become a participator. A spectator is one who watches or observes; an onlooker; an observer; a bystander; someone who watches an activity only and does not take part in it; one who attends and watches a public display.

In a museum at Greenfield Village, Detroit, Michigan, there is a huge steam locomotive. Beside this complicated piece of machinery is a sign showing boiler pressure, size and number of wheels, horsepower, lengths, weight and more. The bottom line indicates that 96 percent of the power generated was used to move the locomotive and only 4 percent was left to pull the load. Someone said that some churches are like that.[7]

We are to become participators. We are to be people who give individually or with others to a common fund or collective effort; people who share something.

One pastor wrote the following creative letter to the congregation:

Football in the fall. Basketball in the winter. Baseball in the spring and summer. This pastor has been an avid sports fan all his life. But I've had it! I quit this sports business once and for all. You can't get me near one of those places again. Do you want to know why?

◆ Every time I went, they asked me for money.

◆ The people with whom I had to sit didn't seem very friendly.

◆ The seats were too hard and not at all comfortable.

◆ I went to many games, but the coach never came to call on me.

◆ The referee made a decision with which I could not agree.

◆ I suspected that I was sitting with some hypocrites—they came to see their friends and what others were wearing rather than to see the game.

◆ Some games went into overtime, and I was late getting home.

◆ The band played some numbers that I had never heard before and didn't even like.

- It seems that the games are scheduled when I want to do other things.

- My parents took me to too many games when I was growing up.

- I don't want to take my children to any games, because I want them to choose for themselves what sport they like best.[8]

BENEFITS OF MAKING A COMMITMENT TO THE FIRST DAY GATHERING

Making a first day gathering commitment to your church, the church in which God has placed you, has many benefits (see Eph. 2:19-21; 3:16; 4:12; 4:14,15; 5:21):

1. Jesus in the midst of His church.

2. The communion table of the Lord is served.

3. The presence of God manifested through dynamic and spirit-filled worship.

4. The power of the Holy Spirit is at work in every service to strengthen and heal.

5. The mind is renewed, cleansed and rebuilt every time it is exposed to the Word and the Spirit.

6. The spiritual inner man is strengthened through prayer, worship and the word.

7. The fellowship of the believers builds relationships and friendships that last a lifetime.

8. The children are loved, instructed and prayed for during every gathering.

9. The wisdom of God revealed in and through the people of God for every circumstance.

10. The preaching of the God's is biblical and balanced.

11. The opportunity to repent of sins and receive forgiveness and cleansing is always available.

12. The is continual encouragement to believe and see God in all seasons of life.

13. The focused confrontation with the spirit of the world.

14. The unified prayers of the church to resist the powers of darkness.

15. The practical principles of the believer's power to live in victory.

16. The worshiping and working together with other believers to reach out and to touch the world around us.

17. The joy of fulfilling God-ordained vision and purpose with other faith-filled people.

18. The receiving of prayer for healing with the anointing of oil by the elders.

19. The pastoral ministry continually administered with wisdom, balance and integrity.

20. The practical and biblical principles on marriage and family taught clearly and consistently.

21. The believer is equipped to be a good steward of his or her talents and finances.

22. The professional person is encouraged in his or her pursuit in the marketplace as a God-given ministry.

23. The youth are challenged to live according to biblical principles and not be squeezed into the world's mold.

24. The power of the Cross and authority of the believer is taught with conviction toward spiritual freedom.

25. The gifts of the Spirit are encouraged and a belief that God still speaks today.

26. The nature of spiritual warfare and the reality of the invisible is instructed clearly.

27. The opportunity to partner with the church in seeing your friends and family find Christ.

28. The beauty of praying together with hundreds of people is faith-building and mountain-moving.

29. The place to be when going through a crisis in life is the gathering of God's people.

30. The passing on to another generation that God's house is worthy of my time every week.

I've just listed 30 beneficial reasons for attending church; however, the greatest reason of all comes from Isaiah 58:13,14 because it is the Lord's promise to you:

> "Keep the Sabbath day holy. Don't pursue your own interests on that day, but enjoy the Sabbath and speak of it with delight as the LORD 's holy day. Honor the LORD in everything you do, and don't follow your own desires or talk idly. If you do this, the LORD will be your delight. I will give you great honor and give you your full share of the inheritance I promised to Jacob, your ancestor. I, the LORD , have spoken!"

I have truly enjoyed spending time with you looking at the seven laws of first things. I would like to conclude our time together with one more challenge: Commit to becoming a doer of these first things and not just a hearer only.

> A great philosopher tells us about a make-believe country where only ducks lived. On Sunday morning, all the ducks came into the church, waddled down the aisle, waddled into their pews and squatted. Then the duck minister came in, took his place behind the pulpit, opened the Duck Bible and read, "Ducks! You have wings, and with wings you can fly like eagles. You can soar into the skies! Ducks! You have wings!" All the ducks yelled, "Amen!" and then they all waddled home.
> Many people are exactly like those ducks. They know the truth but they don't act upon the truth.[9]

Will you?

NOTES

1   Robert J. Morgan, *Stories, Illustrations & Quotes* (Nashville: Thomas Nelson, 2000) p. 70.

2   Ibid., p. 71.

3   George Barna, http://www.barna.org/cgi-bin/PageCategory.asp?CategoryID=10.

4   Paul Kurtz, ed., *Humanist Manifestos I and II* (Buffalo: Prometheus Books, 1982), pp. 10, 13.

5   *Justin Martyr's First Apology, Section 66*, "Weekly Worship of the Christians" http://www.philthompson.net/pages/library/justinap1.html.

6   Charles W. Colson, *The Body* (Dallas: Word Publishing,1992), p. 70.

7   Author Unknown. www.sermonillustrations.com

8   Author Unknown, *At Calvary*, Covington, KY. www.sermonillustrations.com.

9   Jim Burns, *Radical Christianity* (Ventura, Calif.: Regal Books, 1996), p. 57.

Appendix A
Faith Scriptures

Jeremiah 29:11: For I know the thoughts that I think toward you, says the LORD, thoughts of peace and not of evil, to give you a future and a hope.

Matthew 9:28,29: And when He had come into the house, the blind men came to Him. And Jesus said to them, "Do you believe that I am able to do this?" They said to Him, "Yes, Lord." Then He touched their eyes, saying, "According to your faith let it be to you."

Mark 11:24: "Therefore I tell you, whatever you ask for in prayer, believe that you have received it, and it will be yours."

Luke 7:9: When Jesus heard these things, He marveled at him, and turned around and said to the crowd that followed Him, "I say to you, I have not found such great faith, not even in Israel!"

Luke 17:5: And the apostles said to the Lord, "Increase our faith."

Acts 16:5: So the churches were strengthened in the faith, and increased in number daily.

Romans 10:17: So then faith comes by hearing, and hearing by the word of God.

2 Corinthians: It is written: "I believed; therefore I have spoken." With that same spirit of faith we also believe and therefore speak.

Hebrews 11:1,2: What is faith? It is the confident assurance that what we hope for is going to happen. It is the evidence of things we cannot yet see. God gave his approval to people in days of old because of their faith (NLT).

Hebrews 11:6: But without faith it is impossible to please Him, for he who comes to God must believe that He is, and that He is a rewarder of those who diligently seek Him.

Ephesians 1:18: The eyes of your understanding being enlightened; that you may know what is the hope of His calling, what are the riches of the glory of His inheritance in the saints,

Ephesians 3:20: Now glory be to God! By his mighty power at work within us, he is able to accomplish infinitely more than we would ever dare to ask or hope (NLT).

Appendix B
List for Parents

Parents should avoid the following proven ways to drive children away from home and the church:

- Expressing approval only when the child is good
- Threatening the child
- Ridiculing the child
- Screaming at the child
- Being too busy to listen
- Giving the child the silent treatment
- Having a continually critical attitude
- Using the child's name negatively
- Expressing disappointment or disgust for the child's actions
- Breaking the love routine by acting inconsistent in loving the child
- Neglecting or ignoring the child
- Abusing the child physically or psychologically
- Finding fault continually
- Refusing to listen to the child
- Being a poor parental example
- Expressing conditional love
- Expecting the child to do things you didn't or don't do
- Neglecting to be involved in the child's life
- Failing to build family togetherness, pride and loyalty
- Seeking from the child what you should be getting from your spouse
- Allowing negative peer influence

- Being too permissive
- Being overly demanding intellectually, spiritually, physically or emotionally
- Having double standards, one for the parent and one for the child
- Moving or changing standards
- Pressuring the child to be a carbon copy of yourself or someone else
- Expressing disrespect or disappointment
- Exercising unbiblical parenting principles

(Taken from *The Gate Church* by Frank Damazio, chapter 6)